Hiding in Plain Sight

Hebrew Poetry in The Book of Mormon

Compiled by Philip M. Hudson

Copyright 2020 by Philip M. Hudson.

Published 2020.

Printed in the United States of America.

All rights reserved.

No portion of this book may be reproduced, stored in a retrieval system, or transmitted in any form or by any means – electronic, mechanical, photocopy, recording, scanning, or other – except for brief quotations in critical reviews or articles, without the prior written permission of the author.

ISBN 978-1-950647-49-1

Illustrations – Google Images.

This book may be ordered from online bookstores.

Publishing Services by BookCrafters
Parker, Colorado.
www.bookcrafters.net

Table of Contents

Acknowledgements..i
Preface...xi
Introduction...xxxiii

Antithetical Parallel Poetry...1
Synonymous Parallel Poetry...79
Synthetic Parallel Poetry..157
Climactic Parallel Poetry..239
Chiasmus...317

Appendix One..395
Appendix Two...407
About The Author..411
By The Author...413
What More Can I Say?...417

Acknowledgements

The holy scriptures
speak for themselves, because each
Gospel principle carries within itself
its own witness. I hope this book will
cultivate your interest to dig deeper into
the themes woven into the tapestry of
Hebrew poetry, and that as you turn
to the teachings of The Book of
Mormon for guidance, you
will find inspiration
from the Spirit.

My only goal is to help you
to expand your insights into the
telestial mile markers, the terrestrial
truths, and the celestial guidelines that
accompany each of us during our
quest for enlightenment as we
become more familiar with
"the ways of the Jews."
(2 Nephi 25:5).

As I organized
these scriptures, it struck me
just how heavily I have borrowed from
the towering examples of those who, over
the years, have been my mystical mentors,
my sensible chaperones, my spiritual
guides, my surrogate saviors, my
compassionate critics, and
everything in between.

They have been
my avatars, the very
manifestations of deity
in bodily forms, my na'vi, the
visionaries, who communicate
with God on a level to which I
can only aspire, and my tsaddik,
whom I esteem as intuitive
interpreters of biblical
law and scripture.

They are my
divine teachers incarnate.
They have offered listening ears,
extended open arms, lifted my spirits,
shown me the way, stretched my mind,
reinforced my faith, strengthened my
testimony, helped me to discover
my wings, given immaterial
support, and provided
of their means.

They have emboldened me with words of encouragement, cheered me on with wise counsel, taught me humility, been there to steady me, soothed my troubled soul, stepped in to nurture me, led me to fountains of living water, wet my parched lips with inspired counsel, and bound up my wounds.

They may or may not know who they are, or how they have influenced me, but to each of them, I will be eternally grateful.

Preface

I love to
learn by reading The
Book of Mormon, and
when I do, I often think
of St. Hilary, who wrote in the
third century: "Scripture consists
not in what we read, but in what we
understand." While searching for the
passages that would ultimately find
their way onto the pages within this
volume, I sought confirmation by
the Spirit as I discovered the
doctrinal foundations that
lie within the style of
Hebrew poetry.

Within
Hebrew poetry,
I discovered a palate
upon which was revealed a
rich assortment of colors, into
which the prophets had dipped
their brushes, to paint vibrant
portraits upon the canvas
of the Nephite record.

However, the discovery of their renderings has neither proven nor disproven the divine authenticity of The Book of Mormon. Rather, it has facilitated our enjoyment of its inherent beauty, while intensifying our appreciation of the natural appeal of its narrative.

Consequently, when we read The Book of Mormon, we sense that it is virtuous, lovely, of good report, and praiseworthy. It reminds us to heed the counsel of Nephi, to press forward with complete dedication and steadfastness or confidence, with a firm determination in Christ, with a perfect brightness of hope or faith, and with charity or a love of God and of all men. (See 2 Nephi 31:20).

The rich
sprinkling of Hebrew
poetry within its pages
helps us to feast upon the
words of Christ, and to ponder
the doctrines of the kingdom. We
receive the strength to endure one
more day in righteousness. Our eyes
remain fixed upon the prize of the
high calling of Jesus Christ, and
we can more acutely taste the
principles of eternal life,
which is the greatest
of the gifts of
God.

Speaking out of the dust,
Nephi wrote: "Wherefore, hearken,
O my people, which are of the house of
Israel, and give ear unto my words (which)
are plain unto all those that are filled with
the spirit of prophecy. But I give unto you a
prophecy, according to the spirit which is in
me; wherefore I shall prophesy according
to the plainness which hath been with
me from the time that I came out
from Jerusalem with my father;
for behold, my soul delighteth
in plainness unto my people,
that they may learn."
(2 Nephi 25:4).

"My soul delighteth
in the words of Isaiah,
for I came out from Jerusalem,
and mine eyes hath beheld the things
of the Jews, and I know that the Jews do
understand the things of the prophets,
and there is none other people that
understand the things which were
spoken unto the Jews like unto
them, save it be that they are
taught after the manner of
the things of the Jews."
(2 Nephi 25:5).

Nephi exhorts us to read his record as if we had been taught after the manner of the Jews. As members of the House of Israel by either blood or by covenant, our appreciation of the poetry of our forefathers helps us to do just that.

A word about
the discovery within
The Book of Mormon of
chiasmus, which is a particularly
intriguing example of Hebrew poetry.
A Pandora's box of chiasms has been
identified within the text. Some have
been "used in an attempt to uncover
hidden meanings, while others are
treated as evidence of particular
points of view in debates about
Book of Mormon origins."

"Some people use the presence of chiasms within the body of The Book of Mormon as evidence that the prophet Joseph Smith knew about chiasmus. Others see it as evidence that God revealed this literary device to Joseph without his knowledge."

("When are chiasms admissible as evidence?" W. Farrell Edwards & Boyd F. Edwards, B.Y.U. Studies 49:4).

It
is my goal
in this volume
to do none of the
above, but only to help
you to be be taught by the
Spirit, and thru Hebrew poetry
to think like an Israelite, to
more easily ascend to new
plateaus of discovery as
you move onward in
the direction of
your dreams.

It is with love,
then, that I extend
to you the invitation
to savor these selections
of Hebrew poetry that have
been drizzled through
The Book of Mormon
like sugar on a
spice cake.

Introduction

It is remarkabe, not ony that parallel poetry exists in the flowing narrative of The Book of Mormon, but also that it is so universally embedded within the literary contributions of its more than twenty individual authors; moreover, that its subtle occurrence, and particularly chiasmus, was essentially overlooked by its readers for over 150 years. Even careful students of the scriptures have taken for granted its emotional expression.

As it turns out, it is its Hebrew poetry that makes The Book of Mormon easy to read and hard to forget. Its style is an intrinsic witness of its heavenly authenticity, and its structure not only testifies of Jesus Christ, but also of the divine design that our Heavenly Father has for each of us.

The
Book of Mormon
was meant to be read with
an easy grace that is a heavenly
gift, with the Holy Ghost quietly
confirming the testimony of
Jesus Christ, that "as your
Lord and your God
liveth, it is true."
(D&C 17:6).

Readers who
may be familiar with
the poetic passages in this
volume, which is aptly entitled
"Hiding in Plain Sight", may have
taken for granted the care with which
the narrative of The Book of Mormon was
construted. However, its unambiguous style
witnesses that those who were entrusted
to write upon the plates were guided
by the workings of the Spirit. (See
Words of Mormon 1:7).

"And when ye shall receive these things, I would exhort you that ye would ask God, the Eternal Father, in the name of Christ, if these things are not true; and if ye shall ask with a sincere heart, with real intent, having faith in Christ, he will manifest the truth of it unto you, by the power of the Holy Ghost." (Moroni 10:4).

Antithetical Parallel Poetry

in The Book of Mormon

Antithetical parallelism is a literary device that brings together ideas that contrast each other. Rather than saying the same thing twice, antithetically parallel poetry introduces a concept, and then repeats it in opposite terms.

75 Examples of Antithetical Parallel Poetry

"And inasmuch as ye shall keep my commandments, ye shall prosper, and shall be led to a land of promise, yea, even a land which I have prepared for you; yea, a land which is choice above all other lands. And inasmuch as thy brethren shall rebel against thee, they shall be cut off from the presence of the Lord."
(1 Nephi 2:20-21).

"The things which are pleasing unto the world I do not write, but the things which are pleasing unto God and unto those who are not of the world." (1 Nephi 6:5).

"I beheld
that the power of
God was with them,
and also that the wrath
of God was upon all those
that were gathered together
against them to battle."
(1 Nephi 13:18).

"I will work a great
and a marvelous work among the
children of men; a work which shall be
everlasting, either on the one hand or on the
other — either to the convincing of them unto
peace and life eternal, or unto the deliverance
of them to the hardness of their hearts and
the blindness of their minds unto their
being brought down into captivity,
and also into destruction."
(1 Nephi 14:7).

"The things which thou shalt see hereafter thou shalt not write; for the Lord God hath ordained the apostle of the Lamb of God that he should write them."
(1 Nephi 14:25).

"He truly spake many great things unto them, which were hard to be understood, save a man should inquire of the Lord; and they being hard in their hearts, therefore they did not look unto the Lord as they ought." (1 Nephi 15:3).

"I said unto them: Have ye inquired of the Lord? And they said unto me: We have not; for the Lord maketh no such thing known unto us."
(1 Nephi 15:8-9).

"And now my brethren, if ye were righteous and were willing to hearken to the truth, and give heed unto it, that ye might walk uprightly before God, then ye would not murmur because of the truth, and say: Thou speakest hard things against us."
(1 Nephi 16:3).

"And thus we see that by small means the Lord can bring about great things." (1 Nephi 16:29).

"Notwithstanding
we had suffered many
afflictions and much difficulty,
yea, even so much that we cannot
write them all, we were exceedingly
rejoiced when we came to the
seashore; and we called
the place Bountiful."
(1 Nephi 17:6).

"He raiseth up a righteous nation, and destroyeth the nations of the wicked." (1 Nephi 17:37).

"And he leadeth away the righteous into precious lands, and the wicked he destroyeth, and curseth the land unto them for their sakes."
(1 Nephi 17:38).

"Ye are
swift to do iniquity
but slow to remember
the Lord your God."
(1 Nephi 17:45).

"The things which some men esteem to be of great worth, both to the body and soul, others set at naught and trample under their feet." (1 Nephi 19:7).

"Thus saith the Lord,
the Redeemer of Israel, his Holy
One, to him whom man despiseth, to
him whom the nations abhorreth, to
servant of rulers: Kings shall see
and arise, princes also shall
worship, because of the
Lord that is faithful."
(1 Nephi 21:7).

"If iniquity shall abound, cursed shall be the land for their sakes, but unto the righteous it shall be blessed forever." (2 Nephi 1:7).

"Inasmuch as ye shall keep my commandments, ye shall prosper in the land; but inasmuch as ye will not keep my commandments, ye shall be cut off from my presence." (2 Nephi 1:20).

"Ye have accursed
him that he sought power
and authority over you; but
I know that he hath not sought
for power nor authority over you,
but he hath sought the glory
of God, and your own
eternal welfare."
(2 Nephi 1:25).

"Ye say that he hath used sharpness; ye say that he hath been angry with you; but behold, his sharpness was the sharpness of the power of the word of God, which was in him; and that which ye call anger was the truth, according to that which is in God."
(2 Nephi 1:26).

"Behold, if ye will hearken unto the voice of Nephi, ye shall not perish. And if ye will hearken unto him, I leave unto you a blessing, yea, even my first blessing. But if ye will not hearken unto him, I take away my first blessing, yea, even my blessing, and it shall rest upon him."
(2 Nephi 1:28-29).

"For it must needs be, that there is an opposition in all things. If not so, my firstborn in the wilderness, righteousness could not be brought to pass, neither wickedness, neither holiness nor misery, neither good nor bad."
(2 Nephi 2:11).

"And now, my sons, I would that ye should look to the great Mediator, and hearken unto his great commandments; and be faithful unto his words, and choose eternal life, according to the will of his Holy Spirit; And not choose eternal death, according to the will of the flesh and the evil which is therein, which giveth the spirit of the devil power to captivate, to bring you down to hell, that he may reign over you in his own kingdom." (2 Nephi 2:28-29).

"I will raise up a Moses; and I will give power unto him in a rod; and I will give judgment unto him in writing. Yet, I will not loose his tongue, that he shall speak much, for I will not make him mighty in speaking. But I will write unto him my law, by the finger of mine own hand; and I will make a spokesman for him." (2 Nephi 3:17).

"Inasmuch as ye shall keep my commandments ye shall prosper in the land; and inasmuch as ye will not keep my commandments ye shall be cut off." (2 Nephi 4:4).

"When I desire to rejoice, my heart groaneth because of my sins." (2 Nephi 4:19).

"Wilt thou make my path straight before me! Wilt thou not place a stumbling block in my way. But that thou wouldst clear my way before me, and hedge not up my way, but the way of mine enemy.'"
(2 Nephi 4:33).

"They
who are righteous
shall be righteous still,
and they who are filthy
shall be filthy still."
(2 Nephi 9:16).

"And he commandeth
all men that they must repent
and be baptized in his name, having
perfect faith in the Holy One of Israel,
or they cannot be saved in the kingdom
of God. And if they will not repent and
believe in his name, and be baptized in
his name, and endure to the end,
they must be damned; for the
Lord God, the Holy One of
Israel, has spoken it."
(2 Nephi 9:23-24).

"To be carnally-minded is death, and to be spiritually-minded is life eternal." (2 Nephi 9:39).

"O house of Jacob, come ye and let us walk in the light of the Lord; yea, come, for ye have all gone astray, every one to his wicked ways." (2 Nephi 12:5).

"And the loftiness of man shall be bowed down, and the haughtiness of men shall be made low; and the Lord alone shall be exalted." (2 Nephi 12:7).

"It shall come to pass, instead of sweet smell, there shall be stink; and instead of a girdle, a rent; and instead of well-set hair, baldness, and instead of a stomacher, a girdling of sackcloth; burning instead of beauty." (2 Nephi 13:24).

"And the harp, and the viol, the tabret, and pipe, and wine are in their feasts; but they regard not the work of the Lord, neither consider the operation of his hands." (2 Nephi 15:12).

"And the mean man shall be brought down, and the mighty man shall be humbled, and the eyes of the lofty shall be humbled. But the Lord of Hosts shall be exalted in judgment, and God that is holy shall be sanctified in righteousness."
(2 Nephi 15:15-16).

"Go and tell this people – Hear ye indeed, but they understood not; and see ye indeed, but they perceived not."
(2 Nephi 16:9).

"Make the heart of this people fat, and make their ears heavy, and shut their eyes; lest they see with their eyes, and hear with their ears, and understand with their heart, and be converted and be healed." (2 Nephi 16:10).

"Take counsel together, and it shall come to naught; speak the word, and it shall not stand; for God is with us." (2 Nephi 18:10).

"When they
shall say unto you:
Seek unto them that have
familiar spirits, and unto
wizards that peep and mutter;
should not a people seek unto
their God for the living to
hear from the dead?"
(2 Nephi 18:19).

"The people that walked in darkness have seen a great light; they that dwell in the land of the shadow of death, upon them hath the light shined." (2 Nephi 19:2).

"And he shall not judge after the sight of his eyes, neither reprove after the hearing of his ears, but with righteousness shall he judge the poor, and reprove with equity for the meek of the earth; and he shall smite the earth with the rod of his mouth, and with the breath of his lips shall he slay the wicked."
(2 Nephi 21:3-4).

"Wo unto them that call evil good, and good evil, that put darkness for light, and light for darkness, that put bitter for sweet, and sweet for bitter."
(2 Nephi 25:20).

"For if ye would hearken unto the spirit which teacheth a man to pray, ye would know that ye must pray; for the evil spirit teacheth not a man to pray, but teacheth him that he must not pray." (2 Nephi 33:8).

"I shall call them Lamanites that seek to destroy the people of Nephi, and those who are friendly to Nephi I shall call Nephites." (Jacob 1:14).

"How blessed are they who have labored diligently in his vineyard; and how cursed are they who shall be cast out into their own place!" (Jacob 6:3).

"We had many seasons of peace; and we had many seasons of serious war and bloodshed." (Omni 1:3).

"There is nothing which is good save it comes from the Lord; and that which is evil cometh from the devil."
(Omni 1:25)

"Can ye say aught of yourselves? I answer you, Nay. Ye cannot say that ye are even as much as the dust of the earth; yet ye were created out of the dust of the earth; but behold, it belongeth to him who created you."
(Mosiah 2:25).

"For they were a stiffnecked people, quick to do iniquity, and slow to remember the Lord their God." (Mosiah 3:29).

"He commanded them that there should be no contention one with another, but that they should look forward with one eye, having one faith and one baptism, having their hearts knit together in unity and in love one towards another."
(Mosiah 18:21).

"My soul hath been redeemed from the gall of bitterness and bonds of iniquity. I was in the darkest abyss; but now I behold the marvelous light of God. My soul was racked with eternal torment; but I am snatched, and my soul is pained no more." (Mosiah 27:29).

"Now this was a great trial to those that did stand fast in the faith; nevertheless, they were steadfast and immovable in keeping the commandments of God, and they bore with patience the persecution which was heaped upon them."
(Alma 1:25).

"Whatsoever is good cometh from God, and whatsoever is evil cometh from the devil." Alma 5:40).

"Do ye not remember the words which he spake unto Lehi, saying that: Inasmuch as ye shall keep my commandments, ye shall prosper in the land? And again it is said that: Inasmuch as ye will not keep my commandments ye shall be cut off from the presence of the Lord."
(Alma 9:13).

"If they have been righteous, they shall reap the power and deliverance of Jesus Christ; and if they have been evil, they shall reap the damnation of their souls, according to the power and captivation of the devil." (Alma 9:28).

"If ye will repent, ye shall be saved, and if ye will not repent, ye shall be cast off at the last day." (Alma 22:6).

"If ye could be healed by merely casting about your eyes that ye might be healed, would ye not behold quickly, or would ye rather harden your hearts in unbelief, and be slothful, that ye would not cast about your eyes, that ye might perish?"
(Alma 33:21).

"And oh,
What joy, and
what marvelous
light I did behold;
yea, my soul was filled
with joy as exceeding
as was my pain!"
(Alma 36:20).

"Yea, I say unto you, my son, that there could be nothing so exquisite and so bitter as were my pains. Yea, and again I say unto you, my son, that on the other hand, there can be nothing so exquisite and sweet as was my joy." (Alma 36:21).

"I do not say that these things shall be, of myself, because it is not of myself that I know these things; but behold, I know that these things are true because the Lord God has made them known unto me, therefore, I testify that they shall be."
(Helaman 7:29).

"Take ... no thought for the morrow, for the morrow shall take thought for the things of itself." (3 Nephi 13:34).

"Enter ye in at the strait gate; for wide is the gate, and broad is the way, which leadeth to destruction, and many there be who go in thereat."
(3 Nephi 14:13).

"Ye shall not go out with haste, nor go by flight; for the Lord will go before you, and the God of Israel shall be your rearward." (3 Nephi 20:42).

"Enter ye in at the strait gate; for strait is the gate, and narrow is the way that leads to life, and few there be that find it; but wide is the gate, and broad the way which leads to death, and many there be that travel therein."
(3 Nephi 27:33).

"And I did endeavor to preach unto this people, but my mouth was shut, and I was forbidden that I should preach unto them." (Mormon 1:16).

"But behold, this my joy was in vain, for their sorrowing was not unto repentance, because of the goodness of God; but it was rather the sorrowing of the damned, because the Lord would not always suffer them to take happiness in sin." (Mormon 2:13).

"They did not come unto Jesus with broken hearts and contrite spirits, but they did curse God, and wish to die." (Mormon 2:14).

"The strength of the Lord was not with us; yea, we were left to ourselves, that the Spirit of the Lord did not abide in us; therefore we had become weak like unto our brethren." (Mormon 2:26).

"He that believeth and is baptized shall be saved; but he that believeth not shall be damned." (Ether 4:18).

"If there be
no faith among
the children of men,
God can do no miracle
among them; wherefore, he
showed not himself until
after their faith."
(Ether 12:12).

"Thou hast also made our words powerful and great, even that we cannot write them; wherefore, when we write, we behold our weakness, and stumble because of the placing of our words." (Ether 12:25).

"Fools mock, but they shall mourn." (Ether 12:26)

"A bitter fountain cannot bring forth good water; neither can a good fountain bring forth bitter water; wherefore, a man being a servant of the devil cannot follow Christ; and if he follow Christ he cannot be a servant of the devil."
(Moroni 7:11).

"Every thing which inviteth to do good, and to persuade to believe in Christ, is sent forth by the power and gift of Christ; wherefore, ye may know with a perfect knowledge it is of God. But whatsoever thing persuadeth men to do evil, and believe not in Christ, and deny him, and serve not God, then ye may know with a perfect knowledge it is of the devil."
(Moroni 7:16-17)

"Wherefore, if a man have faith, he must needs have hope; for without faith there cannot be any hope." (Moroni 7:42).

"I came into the world, not to call the righteous, but sinners to repentance; the whole need no physician, but they that are sick." (Moroni 8:8).

Synonymous Parallel Poetry

in
The Book of Mormon

Synonymous parallelism
is a literary device that restates
the same idea in different words. It
utilizes the repetition of one idea in a
subsequent line. The first half makes a
statement, and the second half says
the same thing, but with minor
variations. The statements
are juxtaposed, with
similar syntax.

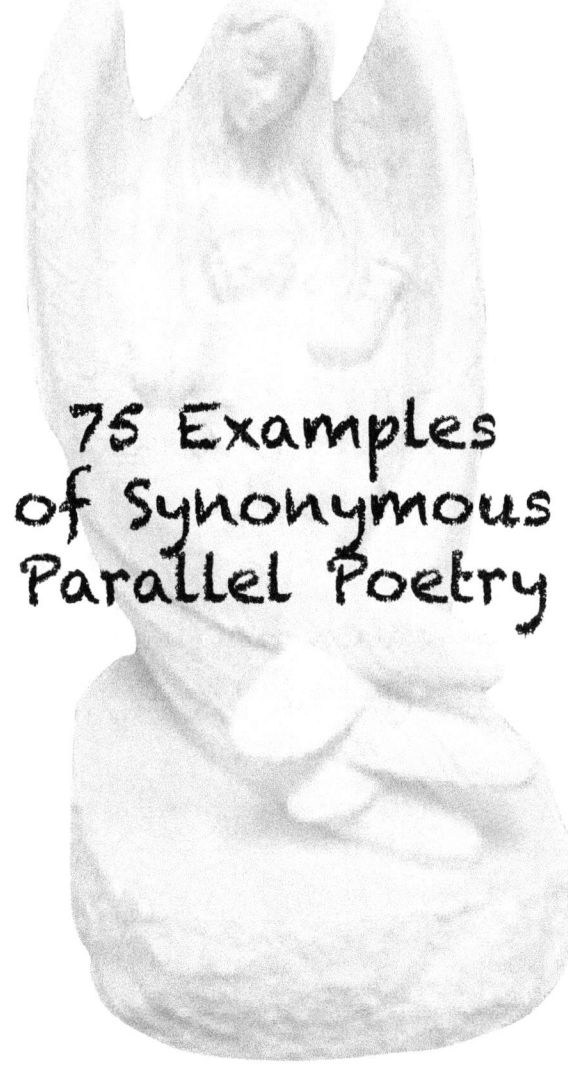

75 Examples of Synonymous Parallel Poetry

"Because of the things which he saw and heard, he did quake and tremble exceedingly ... being overcome with the Spirit and the things which he had seen."
(1 Nephi 1:6-7).

"He was obedient unto the word of the Lord, wherefore, he did as the Lord commanded him." (1 Nephi 2:3).

"They did murmur in many things against their father, because he was a visionary man, and had led them out of the land of Jerusalem, to leave the land of their inheritance, and their gold, and their silver, and their precious things, to perish in the wilderness. And this they said he had done because of the foolish imaginations of his heart."
(1 Nephi 2:11).

"He said that these plates of brass should not perish; neither should they be dimmed any more by time." (1 Nephi 5:19).

"Behold, I have dreamed a dream; or, in other words, I have seen a vision." (1 Nephi 8:2).

"Upon the other plates should be engraven an account of the reign of the kings, and the wars and contentions of my people; wherefore, these plates are for the more part of the ministry; and the other plates are for the more part of the reign of the kings and the wars and contentions of my people." (1 Nephi 9:4).

"I spake unto him as a man speaketh; for I beheld that he was in the form of a man; yet nevertheless, I knew that it was the Spirit of the Lord; and he spake unto me as a man speaketh with another."
(1 Nephi 11:11).

"Behold the Lamb of God, yea, even the Son of the Eternal Father!" (1 Nephi 11:21).

"I looked and beheld the Lamb of God, that he was taken by the people; yea, the Son of the everlasting God was judged of the world."
(1 Nephi 11:32).

"It came to pass that I beheld multitudes gathered together to battle, one against the other; and I beheld wars, and rumors of wars, and great slaughters with the sword among my people."
(1 Nephi 12:2).

"And it came to pass that I saw a mist of darkness on the face of the land of promise; and I saw lightnings, and I heard thunderings, and earthquakes, and all manner of tumultuous noises." (1 Nephi 12:4).

"Behold, the Lord hath created the earth that it should be inhabited; and he hath created his children that they should possess it." (1 Nephi 17:36).

"He ruleth high in the heavens, for it is his throne, and this earth is his footstool." (1 Nephi 17:39).

"Behold, my soul is rent with anguish because of you, and my heart is pained; I fear lest ye shall be cast off forever. Behold, I am full of the Spirit of God, insomuch that my frame has no strength."
(1 Nephi 17:47).

"If God had commanded me to do all things, I could do them. If he should command me that I should say unto this water, be thou earth, it should be earth; and if I should say it, it would be done."
(1 Nephi 17:50).

"The Lord said unto me:
Stretch forth thine hand again
unto thy brethren, and they shall
not wither before thee, but I will shock
them, saith the Lord, and this will I do, that
they may know that I am the Lord their God.
And it came to pass, that I stretched forth
my hand unto my brethren, and they did
not wither before me; but the Lord did
shake them, even according to the
word which he had spoken."
(1 Nephi 17:53-54).

"My parents, being stricken
in years, and having suffered much
grief because of their children, they were
brought down, yea, even upon their sick-beds.
Because of their grief and much sorrow, and
the iniquity of my brethren, they were brought
near even to be carried out of this time to
meet their God; yea, their grey hairs were
about to be brought down to lie low
in the dust; yea, even they were
near to be cast with sorrow
into a watery grave."
(1 Nephi 18:17-18).

"We did begin
to till the earth, and
we began to plant seeds;
yea, we did put all our
seeds into the earth."
(1 Nephi 18:24).

"Behold,
I have refined thee;
I have chosen thee in the
furnace of affliction."
(1 Nephi 20:10).

"In the shadow of his hand hath he hid me, and made me a polished shaft; in his quiver hath he hid me." (1 Nephi 21:2).

"Say to
the prisoners:
Go forth; to them
that sit in darkness:
Show yourselves."
(1 Nephi 21:9).

"I will make all my mountains a way, and my highways shall be exalted." (1 Nephi 21:11).

"Behold, Zion hath said: The Lord hath forsaken me, and my Lord hath forgotten me." (1 Nephi 21:14).

"For shall the prey be taken from the mighty, or the lawful captives delivered?" (1 Nephi 21:24).

"O that ye would awake; awake from a deep sleep, yea, even from the sleep of hell." (2 Nephi 1:13).

"Blessed art thou, and thy seed; for thou shalt inherit the land like unto thy brother Nephi. And thy seed shall be numbered with his seed; and thou shalt be even like unto thy brother, and thy seed like unto his seed; and thou shalt be blessed in all thy days."
(2 Nephi 4:11).

"Yea, I know that God will give liberally to him that asketh. Yea, my God wll give me, if I ask not amiss; therefore I will lift up my voice unto thee; yea, I will cry unto thee, my God, the rock of righteousness. Behold, my voice shall forever ascend up unto thee, my rock and mine everlasting God."
(2 Nephi 4:35).

"I clothe the heavens with blackness, and I make sackcloth their covering." (2 Nephi 7:3).

"I am the Lord thy God, whose waves roared; the Lord of Hosts is my name." (2 Nephi 8:3).

"Pray unto him continually by day, and give thanks unto his holy name by night." (2 Nephi 9:52).

"Wo unto them that call evil good, and good evil, that put darkness for light, and light for darkness, that put bitter for sweet, and sweet for bitter!" (2 Nephi 15:20).

"Praise the Lord;
call upon his name;
declare his doings among
the people; make mention
that his name is exalted."
(2 Nephi 22:4).

"The Jews shall be scattered among all nations; yea, and also Babylon shall be destroyed; wherefore, the Jews shall be scattered by other nations."
(2 Nephi 25:15).

"For it shall come to pass in that day that the churches which are built up, and not unto the Lord, when the one shall say unto the other: Behold, I, I am the Lord's; and the others shall say: I, I am the Lord's; and thus shall every one say that hath built up churches, and not unto the Lord."
(2 Nephi 28:3).

"The things of all nations shall be made known; yea, all things shall be made known unto the children of men." (2 Nephi 30:16).

"And we also had many revelations, and the spirit of much prophecy; wherefore, we knew of Christ and his kingdom, which should come."
(Jacob 1:6).

"As many as would hearken unto the voice of the Lord should also depart out of the land with him, into the wilderness — And it came to pass that he did according as the Lord had commanded him. And they departed out of the land into the wilderness, as many as would hearken unto the voice of the Lord."
(Omni 1:12-13).

"And I do this for a wise purpose; for thus it whispereth me, according to the workings of the Spirit of the Lord which is in me. And now, I do not know all things; but the Lord knoweth all things which are to come; wherefore, he worketh in me to do according to his will." (Words of Mormon 1:7).

"There were
a great number, even so
many that they did not number
them; for they had multiplied
exceedingly and waxed
great in the land."
(Mosiah 2:2).

"This mortal shall put on immortality, and this corruption shall put on incorruption." (Mosiah 16:10).

"They did find a land which had been peopled; yea, a land which was covered with dry bones; yea, a land which had been peopled and which had been destroyed." (Mosiah 21:26).

"They pitched their tents, and began to till the ground, and began to build buildings; yea, they were industrious, and did labor exceedingly." (Mosiah 23:5).

"The Lord seeth fit to chasten his people; yea, he trieth their patience and their faith." (Mosiah 23:21).

"I will stop
the Lamanites
in this valley, that
they come no further
in pursuit of this people."
(Mosiah 24:23).

"Those whom he had sent out to watch the camp of the Amlicites were called Zeram, and Amnor, and Manti, and Limher; these were they who went out with their men to watch the camp of the Amlicites."
(Alma 2:22).

"Do ye not suppose that I know of these things myself? Behold, I testify unto you that I do know that these things whereof I have spoken are true. And how do ye suppose that I know of their surety?" (Alma 5:45).

"He began
to teach the people
in the land of Melek
according to the holy order
of God, by which he had been
called; and he began to teach
the people throughout all
the land of Melek."
(Alma 8:4).

"Now, it was for the sole purpose to get gain, because they received their wages according to their employ, therefore, they did stir up the people to riotings, and all manner of disturbances and wickedness, that they might have more employ, that they might get money according to the suits which were brought before them; therefore, they did stir up the people against Alma and Amulek." (Alma 11:20).

"I will boast of my God, for in his strength I can do all things; yea, behold, many mighty miracles we have wrought in this land, for which we will praise his name forever." (Alma 26:12).

"We will give up
the land of Jershon, which is on
the east by the sea, which joins the land
Bountiful, which is on the south of the land
Bountiful; and this land Jershon is the
land which we will give unto our
brethren for an inheritance."
(Alma 27:22).

"This life is the time for men to prepare to meet God; yea, behold the day of this life is the day for men to perform their labors."
(Alma 34:32).

"O, remember, my son, and learn wisdom in thy youth; yea, learn in thy youth to keep the commandments of God."
(Alma 37:5).

"The soul shall be restored to the body, and the body to the soul; yea, and every limb and joint shall be restored to its body; yea, even a hair of the head shall not be lost; but all things shall be restored to their proper and perfect frame." (Alma 40:23).

"Behold, they do not desire that the Lord their God, who hath created them, should rule and reign over them; notwithstanding his great goodness and his mercy towards them, they do set at naught his counsels, and they will not that he should be their guide."
(Helaman 12:6).

"If ye will repent
and return unto the Lord
your God, I will turn away
mine anger, saith the Lord; yea,
thus saith the Lord, blessed
are they who will repent
and turn unto me."
(Helaman 13:11).

"And many graves shall be opened, and shall yield up many of their dead; and many saints shall appear unto many." (Helaman 14:25).

"The people began
to forget those signs
and wonders which they had
heard, and began to be less and less
astonished at a sign or a wonder from
heaven, insomuch that they began to
be hard in their hearts, and blind
in their minds, and began to
disbelieve all which they
had heard and seen."
(3 Nephi 2:1).

"Surely he hath blessed the house of Jacob, and hath been merciful unto the seed of Joseph." (3 Nephi 5:21).

"They did not sin ignorantly, for they knew the will of God concerning them, for it had been taught unto them; therefore, they did willfully rebel against God." (3 Nephi 6:18).

"I have given you the law and the commandments of my Father, that ye shall believe in me, and that ye shall repent of your sins, and come unto me with a broken heart and a contrite spirit. Behold, ye have the commandments before you, and the law is fulfilled."
(3 Nephi 12:19).

"The Lord hath made bare his holy arm in the eyes of all the nations; and all the ends of the earth shall see the salvation of God." (3 Nephi 16:20).

"My people shall know my name; yea, in that day they shall know that I am he that doth speak." (3 Nephi 20:39).

"I, Mormon, make a record of the things which I have both seen and heard, and call it the Book of Mormon."
(Mormon 1:1)

"I began to be learned somewhat after the manner of the learning of my people, and Ammaron said unto me: I perceive that thou art a sober child, and art quick to observe." (Mormon 1:2).

"Vengeance is mine, and
I will repay; and because
this people repented not after
I had delivered them, behold,
they shall be cut off from
the face of the earth."
(Mormon 3:15).

"And it came to pass that I utterly refused to go up against mine enemies; and I did even as the Lord had commanded me; and I did stand as an idle witness to manifest unto the world the things which I saw and heard, according to the manifestations of the Spirit." (Mormon 3:16).

"It is by the wicked that the wicked are punished; for it is the wicked that stir up the hearts of the children of men unto bloodshed." (Mormon 4:5).

"God is the same yesterday, today, and forever, and in him there is no variableness neither shadow of changing." (Mormon 9:9).

"If ye have imagined up unto yourselves a god who doth vary, and in whom there is shadow of changing, then have ye imagined up unto yourselves a god who is not a God of miracles." (Mormon 9:10).

"Thus, didst thou manifest thyself unto thy disciples; for after they had faith, and did speak in thy name, thou didst show thyself unto them in great power."
(Ether 12:31).

"Every man did cleave unto that which was his own, with his hands, and would not borrow, neither would he lend; and every man kept the hilt of his sword in his right hand." (Ether 14:2).

"And it came to pass, that we did gather in our people as fast as it were possible, that we might get them together in one body."
(Moroni 2:7)

"That which is of God inviteth and enticeth to do good continually; wherefore, every thing which inviteth and enticeth to do good, and to love God, and to serve him, is inspired of God." (Moroni 7:13).

"I am filled
with charity, which is
everlasting love."
(Moroni 8:17).

"Whatsoever thing is good is just and true; wherefore, nothing that is good denieth the Christ, but acknowledgeth that he is." (Moroni 10:6).

Synthetic Parallel Poetry

in
The Book of Mormon

Synthetic parallelism
is a literary device that
ties together related thoughts
to emphasize behaviors, traits, or
similarities. Rather than providing a
contrast, or expressing the same idea
in different words, as antithetial or
synonymous parallelism would do,
the second line of synthetic
parallelism completes the
thought of the first
line.

In general,
synthetic parallelism
consists of two or more
elements, with those that
follow the first adding new or
instructive explanation. It can
also establish a relationship
between actions, when the
second phrase describes
the consequences of
the first phrase.

Its elements build upon each other in a synthesis that is not synonymous or antithetical. Instead, the first line simply states an event, and the second states the conclusion. Together, the parts may convey cause and effect, or the second part may clarify the first.

Synthetic parallel poetry
may also embrace the concept
that one thing is better
than another.

It is a
broad category,
but basically, when the
poetical structure is neither
synonymous, antithetical, nor
climactic, and it does not
follow a chiastic pattern,
it could be considered
to be synthetic.

75 Examples of Synthetic Parallel Poetry

"I, Nephi,
having been
born of goodly
parents, therefore I
was taught somewhat
in all the learning of
my father; and having seen
many afflictions in the course of
my days, nevertheless, having been
highly favored of the Lord in all my
days; yea, having had a great knowledge
of the goodness and the mysteries of God,
therefore I make a record of my proceedings
in my days. Yea, I make a record In the
language of my father, which consists of
the learning of the Jews and the
Language of the Egyptians."
(1 Nephi 1:1-2).

"And after this manner was the language of my father in the praising of his God; for his soul did rejoice, and his whole heart was filled, because of the things which he had seen, yea, which the Lord had shown unto him."
(1 Nephi 1:15).

"Laban hath a record of the Jews and also a genealogy of my forefathers, and they are engraven upon plates of brass."
(1 Nephi 3:3).

"And now, as I have spoken concerning these plates, behold they are not the plates upon which I make a full account of the history of my people; for the plates upon which I make a full account of my people I have given the name of Nephi; wherefore, they are called the plates of Nephi, after mine own name; and these plates also are called the plates of Nephi."
(1 Nephi 9:2).

"And the Spirit said unto me: Behold, what desirest thou? And I said: I desire to behold the things which my father saw. And the Spirit said unto me: Believest thou that thy father saw the tree of which he hath spoken? And I said: Yea, thou knowest that I believe all the words of my father."
(1 Nephi 11:2-5).

"I said unto them: How is it that ye do not keep the commandments of the Lord? How is it that ye will perish, because of the hardness of your hearts?"
(1 Nephi 15:10).

"At that day will they
not rejoice and give praise unto
their everlasting God, their rock
and their salvation? Yea, at that day,
will they not receive the strength and
nourishment from the true vine?
Yea, will they not come unto
the true fold of God?"
(1 Nephi 15:15).

"The guilty taketh the truth to be hard, for it cutteth them to the very center." (1 Nephi 16:2).

"And it came to pass that I, Nephi, did make a bellows wherewith to blow the fire, of the skin of beasts, and after I had made a bellows, that I might have wherewith to blow the fire, I did smite two stones together that I might make fire."
(1 Nephi 17:11).

"Behold, the Lord esteemeth all flesh in one; he that is righteous is favored of God" (1 Nephi 17:35).

"I did liken
all scriptures unto us,
that it might be for our
profit and learning."
(1 Nephi 19:23).

"Mine hand hath also laid the foundation of the earth, and my right hand hath spanned the heavens." (1 Nephi 20:13).

"Thus saith the Lord, even the captives of the mighty shall be taken away, and the prey of the terrible shall be delivered; for I will contend with him that contendeth with thee, and I will save thy children." (1 Nephi 21:25).

"It must needs have been created for a thing of naught; wherefore there would have been no purpose in the end of its creation. Wherefore, this thing must needs destroy the wisdom of God and his eternal purposes, and also the power, and the mercy, and the justice of God."
(2 Nephi 2:12).

"Adam fell, that
men might be,
and men are, that
they might have joy.
And the Messiah cometh
in the fulness of time, that
He might redeem the children
of men from the fall."
(2 Nephi 2:25).

"My soul delighteth in the scriptures, and my heart pondereth them ... My soul delighteth in the things of the Lord; and my heart pondereth continually upon the things which I have seen and heard." (2 Nephi 4:15-16).

"Notwithstanding the great goodness of the Lord, in showing me his great and marvelous works, my heart exclaimeth: O wretched man that I am! Yea, my heart sorroweth because of my flesh; my soul grieveth because of mine inquities." (2 Nephi 4:17).

"I am encompassed about, because of the temptations, and the sins which do so easily beset me. And when I desire to rejoice, my heart groaneth becauses of my sins."
(2 Nephi 4:18).

"He hath filled me with his love, even to the consuming of my flesh." (2 Nephi 4:21).

"He hath heard my cry by day, and he hath given me knowledge by visions in the night-time." (2 Nephi 4:23).

"If I have seen so great things, if the Lord in his condescension unto the children of men hath visited men in so much mercy, why should my heart weep and my soul linger in the valley of sorrow, and my flesh waste away, and my strength slacken, because of mine afflictions?" (2 Nephi 4:26).

"Awake, my soul!
No longer droop in sin.
Rejoice, O my heart, and give
place no more for the
enemy of my soul."
(2 Nephi 4:28).

"O Lord, wilt thou redeem my soul? Wilt thou deliver me out of the hands of mine enemies? Wilt thou make me that I may shake at the appearance of sin? May the gates of hell be shut continually before me, because that my heart is broken and my spirit is contrite! O Lord, wilt thou not shut the gates of thy righteousness before me, that I may walk in the path of the low valley, that I may be strict in the plain road!" (2 Nephi 4:31-32).

"And our spirits must
have become like unto him, and
we become devils, angels to a devil,
to be shut out from the presence of our
God, and to remain with the father of lies, in
misery, like unto himself; yea, to that being who
beguiled our first parents, who transformeth
himself nigh unto an angel of light, and
stirreth up the children of men unto
secret combinations of murder
and all manner of secret
works of darkness."
(2 Nephi 9:9).

"How great the plan of our God! For on the other hand, the paradise of God must deliver up the spirits of the righteous, and the grave deliver up the body of the righteous; and the spirit and the body is restored to itself again, and all men become incorruptible, and immortal, and they are living souls, having a perfect knowledge like unto us in the flesh, save it be that our knowledge shall be perfect." (2 Nephi 9:13).

"But, behold, the righteous, the saints of the Holy One of Israel, they who have believed in the Holy One of Israel, they who have endured the crosses of the world, and despised the shame of it, they shall inherit the kingdom of God, which was prepared for them from the foundation of the world, and their joy shall be full forever." (2 Nephi 9:18).

"Wherefore, he has given a law; and where there is no law given there is no punishment; and where there is no punishment there is no condemnation; and where there is no condemnation the mercies of the Holy One of Israel have claim upon them, because of the atonement; for they are delivered by the power of him. For the atonement satisfieth the demands of his justice upon all those who have not the law given to them, that they are delivered from that awful monster, death and hell."
(2 Nephi 9:25-26).

"Pray unto him continually by day, and give thanks unto his holy name by night." (2 Nephi 9:52).

"For behold, the promises which we have obtained are promises unto us according to the flesh; wherefore, as it has been shown unto me, that many of our children shall perish in the flesh because of unbelief." (2 Nephi 10:2).

"Wherefore, because of their iniquities, destructions, famines, pestilences, and bloodshed shall come upon them, and they who shall not be destroyed shall be scattered among all nations."
(2 Nephi 10:6).

"The kings of the
Gentiles shall be nursing
fathers unto the Gentiles, and
their queens shall become nursing
mothers. Wherefore, the promises of the
Lord are great unto the Gentiles,
for he hath spoken it, and
who can dispute?"
(2 Nephi 10:9).

"He that fighteth against Zion, both Jew and Gentile, both bond and free, both male and female, shall perish; for they are they who are the whore of all the earth, for they who are not for me are against me, saith our God."
(2 Nephi 10:16).

"Wherefore,
I will consecrate
this land unto thy seed, and
them who shall be numbered among
thy seed, forever, for the land of their
inheritance; for it is a choice land, saith
God unto me, above all other land,
wherefore, I will have all men that
dwell thereon that they shall
worship me, saith God."
(2 Nephi 10:19).

"And now, my beloved brethren, seeing that our merciful God has given us so great knowledge concerning these things, let us remember him, and lay aside our sins, and not hang down our heads, for we are not cast off. Nevertheless, we have been driven out of the land of our inheritance, but we have been led to a better land, for the Lord has made the sea our path, and we are upon an isle of the sea." (2 Nephi 10:20).

"For behold,
the Lord God has led away
from time to time from the house
of Israel, according to his will and
pleasure. And now, behold, the Lord
remembereth all them who have
been broken off, wherefore
he remembereth us also."
(2 Nephi 10:22).

"May God raise you from death by the power of the resurrection, and also from everlasting death by the power of the atonement, that ye may be received into the eternal kingdom of God, that ye may praise him through grace divine."
(2 Nephi 10:25).

"And my brother, Jacob, also has seen him as I have seen him; wherefore, I will send their words forth unto my children to prove unto them that my words are true. Wherefore, by the words of three, God hath said, I will establish my word." (2 Nephi 11:3).

"My soul delighteth in the covenants of the Lord which he hath made to our fathers, yea, my soul delighteth in his grace, and in his justice, and power, and mercy in the great and eternal plan of deliverance from death."
(2 Nephi 11:5).

"If there be no Christ, there be no God; and if there be no God, we are not, for there could have been no creation. But there is a God, and he is Christ, and he cometh in the fulness of his own time."
(2 Nephi 11:7).

"Their works were works of darkness, and their doings were doings of abominations." (2 Nephi 25:2).

"Give ear
unto my words;
for because the words
of Isaiah are not plain unto
you, nevertheless, they are plain
unto all those that are filled with
the spirit of prophecy. But I give unto
you a prophecy, according to the spirit
which is in me; wherefore, I shall prophesy
according to the plainness which hath been
with me from the time that I came out
from Jerusalem with my father; for
behold, my soul delighteth in
plainness unto my people,
that they may learn."
(2 Nephi 25:4).

"Doth he cry unto any, saying: Depart from me? Behold, I say unto you, Nay; but he saith: Come unto me all ye ends of the earth, buy milk and honey, without money and without price."
(2 Nephi 26:25).

"Know ye not that there are more nations than one? Know ye not that I, the Lord your God, have created all men, and that I remember those who are upon the isles of the sea; and that I rule in the heavens above and in the earth beneath; and I bring forth my word unto the children of men, yea, even upon all the nations of the earth?" (2 Nephi 29:7).

"Wherefore, the people were desirous to retain in remembrance his name. And whoso should reign in his stead were called by the people, second Nephi, third Nephi, and so forth, according to the reigns of the kings; and thus they were called by the people, let them be of whatever name they would." (Jacob 1:11).

"It came to pass that I, Enos, knowing my father that he was a just man — for he taught me in his language, and also in the nurture and admonition of the Lord — and blessed be the name of my God for it." (Enos 1:1).

"My beloved brethren, I would that ye should come unto Christ, who is the Holy One of Israel, and partake of his salvation, and the power of his redemption. Yea, come unto him, and offer your whole souls as an offering unto him, and continue in fasting and praying, and endure to the end; and as the Lord liveth, ye will be saved." (Omni 1:26).

"Open your ears that ye may hear, and your hearts that ye may understand." (Mosiah 2:9).

"I will visit them in my anger, yea, in my fierce anger will I visit them." (Mosiah 12:1).

"He was wounded for our transgressions; he was bruised for our iniquities; the chastisement of our peace was upon him; and with his stripes we are healed."
(Mosiah 14:5).

"This mortal shal put on immortality, and this corruption shall put on incorruption." (Mosiah 16:10).

"I, Alma, do command you in the language of him who hath commanded me, that ye observe to do the words which I have spoken unto you." (Alma 5:61).

"The word of God was liberal unto all, that none were deprived of the privilege of assembling themselves together to hear the word of God." (Alma 6:5).

"How have ye forgotten the traditions of your fathers? Yea, how soon have ye forgotten the commanments of God!" (Alma 9:8).

"Thou art merciful, O God, for thou hast heard my prayer, even when I was in the wilderness; yea, thou wast merciful when I prayed concerning those who were mine enemies, and thou didst turn them to me."
(Alma 11:4).

"What shall I do that I may have this eternal life of which thou hast spoken? Yea, what shall I do that I may be born of God, having this wicked spirit rooted out of my breast, and receive his Spirit, that I may be filled with joy, that I may not be cast off at the last day? Behold, said he, I will give up all that I possess, yea, I will forsake my kingdom, that I may receive this great joy."
(Alma 22:15).

"According to justice, the plan of redemption could not be brought about, only on conditions of repentance of men in this probationary state, yea, this preparatory state; for except it were for these conditions, mercy could not take effect except it should destroy the work of justice. Now the work of justice could not be destroyed; if so, God would cease to be God." (Alma 42:13).

"Now behold, the Lamanites could not get into their forts of security by any other way save by the entrance, because of the highness of the bank which had been thrown up, and the depth of the ditch which had been dug round about, save it were by the entrance." (Alma 49:18).

"It came to pass that they did set guards over the prisoners of the Lamanites, and did compel them to go forth and bury their dead, yea, and also the dead of the Nephites who were slain; and Moroni placed men over them to guard them while they should perform their labors." (Alma 53:1).

"The Lord had blessed them so long with the riches of the world that they had not been stirred up to anger, to wars, nor to bloodshed; therefore, they began to set their hearts upon their riches; yea, they began to seek to get gain, that they might be lifted up one above another; therefore, they began to commit secret murders, and to rob and to plunder, that they might get gain." (Helaman 6:17).

"The light of the body is the eye; if, therefore, thine eye be single, thy whole body shall be full of light." (3 Nephi 13:22).

"Give not that which is holy unto the dogs, neither cast ye your pearls before swine, lest they trample them under their feet, and turn again, and rend you."
(3 Nephi 14:6).

"Ye are they of whom I said: Other sheep I have which are not of this fold; them also I must bring, and they shall hear my voice; and there shall be one fold, and one shepherd."
(3 Nephi 15:21).

"But I have received a commandment of the Father that I shall go unto them, and that they shall hear my voice, and shall be numbered among my sheep, that there may be one fold and one shepherd; therefore, I go to show myself unto them."
(3 Nephi 16:3).

"For unto us a child is born; unto us a son is given; and the government shall be upon his shoulder; and his name shall be called, Wonderful, Counselor, The Mighty God, the Everlasting Father, The Prince of Peace." (2 Nephi 19:6).

"And all things that he spake have been and shall be, even according to the words which he spake."
(3 Nephi 23:3).

"I have given unto you my gospel, and this is the gospel which I have given unto you — that I came into the world to do the will of my Father, because my Father sent me." (3 Nephi 27:13).

"Turn, all ye Gentiles, from your wicked ways, and repent of your evil doings, of your lyings and deceivings, and of your whoredoms, and of your secret abominations, and your idolatries, and of your murders, and your priestcrafts, and your envyings, and your strifes, and from all your wickedness and abominations, and come unto me, and be baptized in my name, that ye may receive a remission of your sins, and be filled with the Holy Ghost, that ye may be numbered with my people who are of the House of Israel." (3 Nephi 30:2).

"And there were great and marvelous works wrought by the disciples of Jesus, insomuch that they did heal the sick and raise the dead, and cause the lame to walk and the blind to receive their sight, and the deaf to hear; and all manner of miracles did they work among the children of men; and in nothing did they work miracles save it were in the name of Jesus." (4 Nephi 1:5).

"Gadianton robbers, who were among the Lamanites, did infest the land, insomuch that the inhabitants thereof began to hide up their treasures in the earth; and they became slippery, because the Lord had cursed the land, that they could not hold them, nor retain them again. And it came to pass that there were sorceries, and witchcrafts, and magics; and the power of the evil one was wrought upon all the face of the land."
(Mormon 1:18-19).

"And the Lamanites did give unto us the land northward, yea, even to the narrow passage which led into the land southward. And we did give unto the Lamanites all the land southward."
(Mormon 2:39).

"I will show unto you a God of miracles, even the God of Abraham, and the God of Isaac, and the God of Jacob; and it is that same God who created the heavens and the earth, and all things that in them are." (Mormon 9:11).

"And thus they were driven forth; and no monster of the sea could break them, neither a whale that could mar them; and they did have light continually, whether it was above the water or under the water." (Ether 6:10).

"Fools mock, but they shall mourn; and my grace is sufficient for the meek, that they shall take no advantage of your weakness." (Ether 12:26).

"The devil is an enemy unto God, and fighteth against him continually, and inviteth and enticeth to sin, and to do that which is evil continually." (Moroni 7:12).

"The first fruits of repentance is baptism; and baptism cometh by faith unto the fulfilling the commandments; and the fulfilling the commandments bringeth remission of sins; And the remission of sins bringeth meekness, and lowliness of heart; and because of meekness and lowliness of heart cometh the visitation of the Holy Ghost, which Comforter filleth with hope and perfect love, which love endureth by diligence unto prayer, until the end shall come, when all the saints shall dwell with God."
(Moroni 8:25-26).

Climactic Parallel Poetry

in
The Book of Mormon

Climactic
parallel poetry
utilizes words that are
repeated in successive lines,
with additional information
that enlarges the meaning,
until the climactic theme
that had been initiated
in the first line
is stated.

75 Examples of Climactic Parallel Poetry

"He came down by the borders near the shore of the Red Sea; and he traveled in the wilderness in the borders which are nearer the Red Sea; and he did travel in the wilderness with his family." (1 Nephi 2:5).

"I will go and do the things which the Lord hath commanded, for I know that the Lord giveth no commandments unto the children of men, save he shall prepare a way for them that they may accomplish the thing which he commandeth them."
(1 Nephi 3:7).

"How is it that ye have forgotten that ye have seen an angel of the Lord? Yea, and how is it that ye have forgotten what great things the Lord hath done for us, in delivering us out of the hands of Laban, and also that we should obtain the record? Yea, and how is it that ye have forgotten that the Lord is able to do all things according to his will, for the children of men, if it so be that they exercise faith in him? Wherefore, let us be faithful to him."
(1 Nephi 7:10-12).

"The Lord knoweth all things from the beginning; wherefore, he prepareth a way to accomplish all his works among the children of men; for behold, he hath all power unto the fulfilling of all his words."
(1 Nephi 9:6).

"He spake unto them concerning the Jews — That after they should be destroyed, even that great city Jerusalem, and many be carried away captive into Babylon, according to the own due time of the Lord, they should return again, yea, even be brought back out of captivity; and after they should be brought back out of captivity they should possess again the land of their inheritance."
(1 Nephi 10:2-3).

"For he that diligently seeketh shall find; and the mysteries of God shall be unfolded unto them, by the power of the Holy Ghost, as well in these times as in times of old, and as well in times of old as in times to come; wherefore, the course of the Lord is one eternal round."
(1 Nephi 10:19).

"Wherefore, if they should die in their wickedness they must be cast off also, as to the things which are spiritual, which are pertaining to righteousness; wherefore, they must be brought to stand before God, to be judged of their works; and if their works have been filthiness they must needs be filthy; and if they be filthy it must needs be that they cannot dwell in the kingdom of God; if so, the kingdom of God must be filthy also."
(1 Nephi 15:33).

"Laman and Lemuel and the sons of Ishmael did begin to murmur exceedingly, because of their sufferings and afflictions in the wilderness; and also my father began to murmur against the Lord his God; yea, and they were all exceedingly sorrowful, even that they did murmur against the Lord."
(1 Nephi 16:20).

"We knew that
ye could not construct a
ship, for we knew that ye were
lacking in judgment; wherefore,
thou canst not accomplish
so great a work."
(1 Nephi 17:19).

"And it came
to pass that according to
his word he did destroy them;
and according to his word he did
lead them; and according to his
word he did do all things for
them; and there was not
any thing done save it
were by his word."
(1 Nephi 17:31).

"I, Nephi, did not work the timbers after the manner which was learned by men, neither did I build the ship after the manner of men; but I did build it after the manner which the Lord had shown unto me; wherefore, it was not after the manner of men."
(1 Nephi 18:2).

"We did begin to till the earth, and we began to plant seeds; yea, we did put all our seeds into the earth, which we had brought from the land of Jerusalem. And it came to pass that they did grow exceedingly; wherefore, we were blessed in abundance."
(1 Nephi 18:22).

"When that day cometh, saith the prophet, that they no more turn aside their hearts against the Holy One of Israel, then will he remember the covenants which he made to their fathers. Yea, then will he remember the isles of the sea; yea, and all the people who are of the house of Israel, will I gather in, saith the Lord, according to the words of the prophet Zenos, from the four quarters of the earth. Yea, and all the earth shall see the salvation of the Lord, saith the prophet; every nation, kindred, tongue and people shall be blessed."
(1 Nephi 19:15-17).

"Hear ye the words of the prophet, ye who are a remnant of the house of Israel, a branch who have been broken off; hear ye the words of the prophet, which were written unto all the house of Israel, and liken them unto yourselves, that ye may have hope as well as your brethren from whom ye have been broken off; for after this manner has the prophet written."
(1 Nephi 19:24).

"O that thou hadst hearkened to my commandments — then had thy peace been as a river, and thy righteousness as the waves of the sea."
(1 Nephi 20:18).

"And they thirsted not; he led them through the deserts; he caused the waters to flow out of the rock for them; he clave the rock also and the waters gushed out."
(1 Nephi 20:21).

"We have obtained a land of promise, a land which is choice above all other lands; a land which the Lord God hath covenanted with me should be a land for the inheritance of my seed. Yea, the Lord hath covenanted this land unto me, and to my children forever."
(2 Nephi 1:5).

"O that ye would awake; awake from a deep sleep, yea, even from the sleep of hell, and shake off the awful chains by which ye are bound, which are the chains which bind the children of men, that they are carried away captive down to the eternal gulf of misery and woe. Awake! and arise from the dust, and hear the words of a trembling parent."
(2 Nephi 1:13-14).

"Men are instructed sufficiently that they know good from evil. And the law is given unto men. And by the law no flesh is justified; or, by the law men are cut off. Yea, by the temporal law they were cut off; and also, by the spiritual law they perish from that which is good, and become miserable forever. Wherefore, redemption cometh in and through the Holy Messiah."
(2 Nephi 2:5-6).

"The wolf also shall dwell with the lamb, and the leopard shall lie down with the kid, and the calf and the young lion and fatling together; and a little child shall lead them. And the cow and the bear shall feed; their young ones shall lie down together; and the lion shall eat straw like the ox. And the sucking child shall play on the hole of the asp, and the weaned child shall put forth his hand on the cockatrice's den. They shall not hurt nor destroy in all my holy mountain, for the earth shall be full of the knowledge of the Lord, as the waters cover the sea."
(2 Nephi 2:6-9).

"If ye shall say there is no law, ye shall also say there is no sin. If ye shall say there is no sin, ye shall also say there is no righteousness. And if there be no righteousness there be no happiness. And if there be no righteousness nor happiness there be no punishment nor misery. And if these things are not there is no God. And if there is no God we are not, neither the earth; for there could have been no creation of things, neither to act nor to be acted upon; wherefore, all things must have vanished away."
(2 Nephi 2:13).

"He said unto Eve, yea, even that old serpent, who is the devil, who is the father of all lies, wherefore, he said: Partake of the forbidden fruit, and ye shall not die, but ye shall be as God, knowing good and evil."
(2 Nephi 2:18).

"Men are feee according to the flesh; and all things are given them which are expedient unto man. And they are free to choose liberty and eternal life, through the great Mediator of all men, or to choose captivity and death, according to the captivity and power of the devil; for he seeketh that all men might be miserable like unto himself."
(2 Nephi 2:27).

"And upon these I write the things of my soul, and many of the scriptures which are engraven upon the plates of brass. For my soul delighteth in the scriptures, and my heart pondereth them, and writeth them for the learning and the profit of my children. Behold, my soul delighteth in the things of the Lord; and my heart pondereth continually upon the things which I have seen and heard."
(2 Nephi 4:15-16).

"Rejoice,
O my heart, and
cry unto the Lord, and
say: O Lord, I will praise
thee forever; Yea, my soul
will rejoice in thee, my
God, and the rock
of my salvation."
(2 Nephi 4:30).

"And we did take our tents and whatsoever things were possible for us, and did journey in the wilderness for the space of many days. And after we had journeyed for the space of many days, we did pitch our tents."
(2 Nephi 5:7).

"The Lord God said unto me: They shall be a scourge unto thy seed, to stir them up in remembrance of me; and inasmuch as they will not remember me, and hearken unto my words, they shall scourge them, even unto destruction."
(2 Nephi 5:25).

"As death hath passed upon all men, to fulfil the merciful plan of the great Creator, there must needs be a power of resurrection, and the resurrection must needs come unto man by reason of the fall; and the fall came by reason of transgression; and because man became fallen they were cut off from the presence of the Lord. Wherefore, it must needs be an infinite atonement."
(2 Nephi 9:6-7).

"And this death of
which I have spoken, which is
the spiritual death, shall deliver
up its dead; which spiritual death
is hell; wherefore, death and hell must
deliver up their dead, and hell must deliver
up its captive spirits, and the grave must
deliver up its captive bodies, and the
bodies and the spirits of men will
be restored one to the other;
and it is by the power of
the resurrection of the
Holy One of Israel."
(2 Nephi 9:12).

"He has given
a law; and where
there is no law given
there is no punishment; and
where there is no punishment
there is no condemnation; and
where there is no condemnation
the mercies of the Holy One of
Israel have claim upon them,
because of the atonement;
for they are delivered by
the power of him."
(2 Nephi 9:25).

"The Atonement
satisfieth the demands of
his justice upon all those who
have not the law given to them,
that they are delivered from that
awful monster, death and hell, and
the devil, and the lake of fire and
brimstone, which is endless torment;
and they are restored to that God
who gave them breath, which is
the Holy One of Israel."
(2 Nephi 9:26).

"It must
needs be expedient that
Christ ... should come among
the Jews, among those who are
the more wicked part of the world;
and they shall crucify him — for thus
it behooveth our God, and there is
none other nation on earth that
would crucify their God."
(2 Nephi 10:3).

"The light of Israel shall be for a fire, and his Holy One for a flame, and shall burn and shall devour his thorns and his briers in one day." (2 Nephi 20:17).

"And he shall set up an ensign for the nations, and shall assemble the outcasts of Israel, and gather together the dispersed of Judah from the four corners of the earth."
(2 Nephi 21:12).

"The stars of heaven and the constellations thereof shall not give their light; the sun shall be darkened in his going forth, and the moon shall not cause her light to shine." (2 Nephi 23:10).

"And he shall set up an ensign for the nations, and shall assemble the outcasts of Israel, and gather together the dispersed of Judah from the four corners of the earth." (2 Nephi 21:12).

"The stars of heaven and the constellations thereof shall not give their light; the sun shall be darkened in his going forth, and the moon shall not cause her light to shine." (2 Nephi 23:10).

"Notwithstanding we
believe in Christ, we keep the
law of Moses, and look forward
with steadfastness unto Christ, until
the law shall be fulfilled. For, for this
end was the law given ... By knowing
the deadness of the law, (we) look
forward unto that life which is
in Christ, and know for what
end the law was given."
(2 Nephi 25:24-27).

"The right way is to believe in Christ and deny him not; for by denying him ye also deny the prophets and the law. And now behold, I say unto you that the right way is to believe in Christ, and deny him not; and Christ is the Holy One of Israel."
(2 Nephi 25:29).

"Righteousness shall be the girdle of his loins, and faithfulness the girdle of his reins." (2 Nephi 30:11).

"I glory in plainness; I glory in truth. I glory in my Jesus, for he hath redeemed my soul from hell." (2 Nephi 33:6).

"Seek not to counsel the Lord, but to take counsel from his hand. For behold, ye yourselves know that he counseleth in wisdom, and in justice, and in great mercy, over all his works." (Jacob 4:10).

"And my soul hungered; and I kneeled down before my Maker, and I cried unto him in mighty prayer and supplication for mine own soul; and all the day long did I cry unto him; yea, and when the night came I did still raise my voice high that it reached the heavens. And there came a voice unto me, saying: Enos, thy sins are forgiven thee, and thou shalt be blessed."
(Enos 1:4-5).

"When ye are in the service of your fellow beings, ye are only in the service of your God." (Mosiah 2:17).

"They have taught their children that they should hate them, and that they should murder them, and that they should rob and plunder them, and do all they could to destroy them; therefore, they have an eternal hatred towards the children of Nephi." (Mosiah 10:17).

"I command you to bring Abinadi hither, that I may slay him, for he has said these things that he might stir up my people to anger one with another, and to raise contentions among my people; therefore, I will slay him." (Mosiah 11:28).

"Having gone according to their own carnal wills and desires; having never called upon the Lord while the arms of mercy were extended towards them; for the arms of mercy were extended towards them, and they would not; they being warned of their iniquities and yet they would not depart from them; and they were commanded to repent and yet they would not repent."
(Mosiah 16:12).

"O king, if thou hast not found me to be an unprofitable servant, or if thou hast hitherto listened to my words in any degree, and they have been of service to thee, even so I desire that thou wouldst listen to my words at this time, and I will be thy servant and deliver this people out of bondage." (Mosiah 22:4).

"Behold, the Lord hath heard the prayers of his people, and also the prayers of his servant, Alma, who is thy father; for he has prayed with much faith concerning thee that thou mightest be brought to the knowledge of the truth; therefore, for this purpose have I come to convince thee of the power and authority of God, that the prayers of his servants might be answered according to their faith." (Mosiah 27:14).

"They did wax strong in love towards Mosiah; yea, they did esteem him more than any other man; for they did not look upon him as a tyrant who was seeking for gain, yea, for that lucre which doth corrupt the soul; for he had not exacted riches of them, neither had he delighted in the shedding of blood; but he had established peace in the land, and he had granted unto his people that they should be delivered from all manner of bondage; therefore, they did esteem him, yea, exceedingly, beyond measure." (Mosiah 29:40).

"Ye workers of iniquity; ye that are puffed up in the vain things of the world, ye that have professed to have known the ways of righteousness, nevertheless have gone astray, as sheep having no shepherd, notwithstanding a shepherd hath called after you and is still calling after you, but ye will not hearken unto his voice!" (Alma 5:37).

"And he will take upon him death, that he may loose the bands of death which bind his people; and he will take upon him their infirmities, that his bowels may be filled with mercy, according to the flesh, that he may know according to the flesh how to succor his people according to their infirmities."
(Alma 7:12).

"In the eleventh year of the reign of the judges over the people of Nephi, on the fifth day of the second month, there having been much peace in the land of Zarahemla, there having been no wars nor contentions for a certain number of years, even until the fifth day of the second month in the eleventh year, there was a cry of war heard throughout the land." (Alma 16:1).

"As the preaching of the word had a great tendency to lead the people to do that which was just; yea, it had had more powerful effect upon the minds of the people than the sword, or anything else, which had happened unto them, therefore Alma thought it was expedient that they should try the virtue of the word of God."
(Alma 31:5).

"It is well that ye are cast out of your synagogues, that ye may be humble, and that ye may learn wisdom; for it is necessary that ye should learn wisdom; for it is because that ye are cast out, that ye are despised of your brethren because of your exceeding poverty, that ye are brought to a lowliness of heart, for ye are necessarily brought to be humble." (Alma 32:12).

"Because ye are compelled to be humble blessed are ye; for a man sometimes, if he is compelled to be humble, seeketh repentance; and now surely, whosoever repenteth shall find mercy; and he that findeth mercy and endureth to the end, the same shall be saved." (Alma 32:13).

"Because ye were compelled to be humble ye were blessed; do ye not suppose that they are more blessed who truly humble themselves because of the word?" (Alma 32:14).

"I would not that ye think that I know of myself; not of the temporal, but of the spiritual, not of the carnal mind, but of God."
(Alma 36:4).

"Thus, we see that
all mankind were fallen, and
they were in the grasp of justice;
yea, the justice of God, which
consigned them forever to be
cut off from his presence."
(Alma 42:14).

"Many of the Lamanites did go into the land northward; and also Nephi and Lehi went into the land northward, to preach unto the people." (Helaman 10:6).

"Some were lifted up in pride, and others were exceedingly humble; some did return railing for railing, while others would receive railing and persecution and all manner of afflictions, and would not turn and revile again, but were humble and penitent before God."
(3 Nephi 6:13).

"There were some who were carried away in the whirlwind; and whither they went no man knoweth, save they know that they were carried away."
(3 Nephi 8:16).

"Many have testified of these things at the coming of Christ, and were aslain because they testified of these things." (3 Nephi 10:15).

"Because of this great thing which my people, the Nephites, had done, they began to boast in their own strength, and began to swear before the heavens that they would avenge themselves of the blood of their brethren who had been slain by their enemies. And they did swear by the heavens, and also by the throne of God, that they would go up to battle against their enemies, and would cut them off from the face of the land." (Mormon 3:9-10).

"Behold, I had led them, notwithstanding their wickedness, I had led them many times to battle, and had loved them, according to the love of God which was in me, with all my heart; and my soul had been poured out in prayer unto my God all the day long for them; nevertheless, it was without faith, because of the hardness of their hearts."
(Mormon 3:12)

"I am the same who hideth
up this record unto the Lord; the
plates thereof are of no worth, because
of the commandment of the Lord. For
he truly saith that no one shall have
them to get gain; but the record
thereof is of great worth; and
whoso shall bring it to light,
him will the Lord bless."
(Mormon 8:14).

"They were built after a manner that they were exceedingly tight, even that they would hold water like unto a dish; and the bottom thereof was tight like unto a dish; and the sides thereof were tight like unto a dish; and the ends thereof were peaked; and the top thereof was tight like unto a dish; and the length thereof was the length of a tree; and the door thereof, when it was shut, was tight like unto a dish."
(Ether 2:17)

"Whatsoever thing persuadeth men to do good is of me; for good cometh of none save it be of me. I am the same that leadeth men to all good." (Ether 4:12).

"If men come unto me I will show unto them their weakness. I give unto men weakness that they may be humble; and my grace is sufficient for all men that humble themselves before me; for if they humble themselves before me, and have faith in me, then will I make weak things become strong unto them."
(Ether 12:27).

"Thou hast prepared a house for man, yea, even among the mansions of thy Father, in which man might have a more excellent hope; wherefore man must hope, or he cannot receive an inheritance in the place which thou hast prepared."
(Ether 12:32).

"But he repented not, neither his fair sons nor daughters; neither the fair sons and daughters of Cohor; neither the fair sons and daughters of Corihor; and in fine, there were none of the fair sons and daughters upon the face of the whole earth who repented of their sins." (Ether 13:17).

"There began to be a great curse upon all the land because of the iniquity of the people, in which, if a man should lay his tool or his sword upon his shelf, or upon the place whither he would keep it, behold, upon the morrow he could not find it, so great was the curse upon the land." (Ether 14:1).

"If a man being evil giveth a gift, he doeth it grudgingly; wherefore it is counted unto him the same as if he had retained the gift; wherefore he is counted evil before God." (Moroni 7:8).

"God will show unto you, with power and great glory at the last day, that they are true, and if they are true has the day of miracles ceased? Or have angels ceased to appear unto the children of men? Or has he withheld the power of the Holy Ghost from them? Or will he, so long as time shall last, or the earth shall stand, or there shall be one man upon the face thereof to be saved?" (Moroni 7:35-36).

"None is acceptable before God, save the meek and lowly in heart; and if a man be meek and lowly in heart, and confess by the power of the Holy Ghost that Jesus is the Christ, he must needs have charity; for if he have not charity he is nothing; wherefore he must needs have charity ... Wherefore, my beloved brethren, if ye have not charity, ye are nothing, for charity never faileth. Wherefore, cleave unto charity, which is the greatest of all."
(Moroni 7:44 & 46).

"Yea, come unto Christ, and be perfected in him, and deny yourselves of all ungodliness; and if ye shall deny yourselves of all ungodliness, and love God with all your might, mind and strength, then is his grace sufficient for you, that by his grace ye may be perfect in Christ; and if by the grace of God ye are perfect in Christ, ye can in nowise deny the power of God." (Moroni 10:32).

"If ye by the grace of God are perfect in Christ, and deny not his power, then are ye sanctified in Christ by the grace of God, through the shedding of the blood of Christ, which is in the covenant of the Father unto the remission of your sins, that ye become holy, without spot." (Moroni 10:33).

Chiasmus
in
The Book of Mormon

Chiasmus is the
intentional reversal of the
words in a repetition. The idea of
line one is repeated in reverse order.
If the second line of parallel verse
is inverted, that is to say, if its
last element is placed first,
and the first, last, then
a chiasm is created.

75 Examples of Chiasmus

"I, Nephi, do not make a full account of the things which my father hath written, for he hath written many things which he saw in visions and in dreams; and he also hath written many things which he prophesied and spake unto his children, of which I shall not make a full account."
(1 Nephi 1:16).

"I shall make an account
of my proceedings in my days.
Behold, I make an abridgement of the
record of my father, upon plates which
I have made with mine own hands;
wherefore, after I have abridged
the record of my father then
will I make an account
of mine own life."
(1 Nephi 1:17).

"He departed into the wilderness. And he left his house, and the land of his inheritance, and his gold, and his silver, and his precious things, and took nothing with him, save it were his family, and provisions, and tents, and departed into the wilderness." (1 Nephi 2:4).

"Thy brothers murmur, saying it is a hard thing which I have required of them; but behold I have not required it of them, but it is a commandment of the Lord. Therefore go, my son, and thou shalt be favored of the Lord, because thou hast not murmured."
(1 Nephi 3:5-6).

"Let us be faithful in keeping the commandments of the Lord; therefore, let us go down to the land of our father's inheritance, for behold he left gold and silver, and all manner of riches. And all this he hath done because of the commandments of the Lord."
(1 Nephi 3:16).

"And now I, Nephi, do not give the genealogy of my fathers in this part of my record; neither at any time shall I give it after upon these plates which I am writing; for it is given in the record which has been kept by my father; wherefore, I do not write it in this work."
(1 Nephi 6:1).

"For he that diligently seeketh shall find; and the mysteries of God shall be unfolded unto them, by the power of the Holy Ghost, as well in these times as in times of old, and as well in times of old as in times to come; wherefore, the course of the Lord is one eternal round."
(1 Nephi 10:19).

"And I looked and beheld the Lamb of God, that he was taken by the people; yea, the Son of the everlasting God was judged of the world; and I saw and bear record."
(1 Nephi 11:32).

"And while the angel spake these words, I beheld and saw that the seed of my brethren did contend against my seed, according to the word of the angel; and because of the pride of my seed, and the temptations of the devil, I beheld that the seed of my brethren did overpower the people of my seed." (1 Nephi 12:19).

"The time cometh
that he shall manifest
himself unto all nations,
both unto the Jews and also
unto the Gentiles; and after he has
manifested himself unto the Jews and
also unto the Gentiles, then he shall
manifest himself unto the Gentiles
and also unto the Jews, and
the last shall be first, and
the first shall be last."
(1 Nephi 13:42).

"Wherefore, I, Nephi, did exhort them to give heed unto the word of the Lord; yea, I did exhort them with all the energies of my soul, and with all the faculty which I possessed, that they would give heed to the word of God." (1 Nephi 15:25).

"It came to pass that as I, Nephi, went forth to slay food, behold, I did break my bow, which was made of fine steel; and after I did break my bow, behold, my brethren were angry with me because of the loss of my bow, for we did obtain no food." (1 Nephi 16:18).

"And I will also be
your light in the wilderness;
and I will prepare the way before
you, if it so be that ye shall keep my
commandments; wherefore, inasmuch as ye
shall keep my commandments ye shall
be led towards the promised land;
and ye shall know that it is
by me that ye are led."
(1 Nephi 17:13).

"I, Nephi, said many things
unto my brethren, insomuch that
they were confounded and could not
contend against me; neither durst they lay
their hands upon me nor touch me with their
fingers, even for the space of many days. Now
they durst not do this lest they should
wither before me, so powerful was
the Spirit of God; and thus it
had wrought upon them."
(1 Nephi 17:52).

"Hearken, O ye house of Israel, all ye that are broken off and are driven out because of the wickedness of the pastors of my people; yea, all ye that are broken off, that are scattered abroad, who are of my people, O house of Israel." (1 Nephi 21:1).

"Because of the righteousness of his people, Satan has no power; wherefore, he cannot be loosed for the space of many years; for he hath no power over the hearts of the people, for they dwell in righteousness."
(1 Nephi 22:26).

"Awake, my soul!
No longer droop in sin. Rejoice,
O my heart, and give place no more for
the enemy of my soul. Do not anger again
because of mine enemies. Do not slacken
my strength beause of mine afflictions.
Rejoice, O my heart, and cry unto the
Lord, and say: O Lord, I will praise
thee forever; yea, my soul will
rejoice in thee, my God, and
the rock of my salvation."
(2 Nephi 4:28-30).

"I will not put my trust in the arm of flesh; for I know that cursed is he that putteth his trust in the arm of flesh. Yea, cursed is he that putteth his trust in man, or maketh flesh his arm."
(2 Nephi 4:34).

"The words of the Lord had been fulfilled unto my brethren, which he spake concerning them, that I should be their ruler and their teacher. Wherefore, I had been their ruler and their teacher, according to the commandments of the Lord."
(2 Nephi 5:19).

"For shall the prey be taken from the mighty, or the lawful captive delivered? But thus saith the Lord: Even the captives of the mighty shall be taken away; and the prey of the terrible shall be delivered; for the Mighty God shall deliver his covenant people. For thus saith the Lord: I will contend with them that contendeth with thee." (2 Nephi 6:16-17).

"O how great the holiness of our God! For he knoweth all things, and there is not anything save he knows it." (2 Nephi 9:20).

"O that cunning plan of the evil one! O the vainness, and the frailties and the foolishness of men! When they are learned they think they are wise, and they hearken not unto the counsel of God for they set it aside supposing they know of themselves. Wherefore their wisdom is foolishness and it profiteth them not, and they shall perish. But to be learned is good, if they hearken unto the counsels of God."
(2 Nephi 9:28-29).

"Therefore, is the anger of the Lord kindled against his people, and he hath stretched forth his hand against them, and hath smitten them, and the hills did tremble, and their carcasses were torn in the midst of the streets. For all this, his anger is not turned away, but his hand is stretched out still." (2 Nephi 15:25).

"Make the heart of this people
fat, and make their ears heavy, and
shut their eyes — lest they see with their
eyes, and hear with their ears, and
understand with their heart, and
be converted and be healed."
(2 Nephi 16:10).

"Behold, God is my salvation; I will trust, and not be afraid, for the Lord Jehovah is my strength and my song; he also has become my salvation." (2 Nephi 22:2).

"How art thou fallen from heaven, O Lucifer, son of the morning! Art thou cut down to the ground, which did weaken the nations! For thou hast said in thy heart: I will ascend into heaven, I will exalt my throne above the stars of God: I will sit also upon the mount of the congregation, in the sides of the north; I will ascend above the heights of the clouds; I will be like the Most High. Yet thou shalt be brought down to hell, to the sides of the pit."
(2 Nephi 24:12-15).

"Rejoice not thou, whole Palestina, because the rod of him that smote thee is broken; for out of the serpent's root shall come forth a cockatrice, and his fruit shall be a fiery flying serpent. And the firstborn of the poor shall feed, and the needy shall lie down in safety; and I will kill thy root with famine, and he shall slay thy remnant. Howl, O gate; cry, O city; thou, whole Palestina, art dissolved, for there shall come from the north a smoke, and none shall be alone in his appointed times."
(2 Nephi 24:29-31).

"And others will he pacify, and lull them away into carnal security, that they will say: All is well in Zion; yea, Zion prospereth, all is well, and thus, the devil cheateth their souls, and leadeth them away carefully down to hell."
(2 Nephi 28:21).

"The Jews shall have the words of the Nephites, and the Nephites shall have the words of the Jews; and the Nephites and the Jews shall have the words of the lost tribes of Israel; and the lost tribes of Israel shall have the words of the Nephites and the Jews." (2 Nephi 29:13).

"By the power of the word, man came upon the face of the earth, which earth was created by the power of his word. Wherefore, if God being able to speak and the world was, and to speak and man was created, O then, why not able to command the earth, or the workmanship of his hands upon the face of it, according to his will and pleasure?" (Jacob 4:9).

"Thy faith
hath made the whole.
Now it came to pass that when
I had heard these words, I began
to feel a desire for the welfare of my
brethren, the Nephites; wherefore, I did pour
out my whole soul unto God for them ... And
I prayed unto him with many long strugglings
for my brethren, the Lamanites. And it came
to pass that after I had prayed and labored
with all diligence, the Lord said unto me:
I will grant unto thee according to thy
desires, because of thy faith."
(Enos 1:8,9 & 11,12).

"And I soon go to the place of my rest, which is with my Redeemer; for I know that in him I shall rest. And I rejoice in the day when my mortal shall put on immortality, and shall stand before him; then shall I see his face with pleasure, and he will say unto me: Come unto me, ye blessed, there is a place prepared for you in the mansions of my Father."
(Enos 1:27).

"As many as are not stiffnecked and have faith, have communion with the Holy Spirit, which maketh manifest unto the children of men, according to their faith." (Jarom 1:4).

"They discovered a people, who were called the people of Zarahemla. Now, there was great rejoicing among the people of Zarahemla; and also Zarahemla did rejoice exceedingly, because the Lord had sent the people of Mosiah with the plates of brass which contained the record of the Jews." (Omni 1:14).

"For this multitude being so great that King Benjamin could not teach them all within the walls of the temple, therefore, he caused a tower to be erected, that thereby his people might hear the words which he should speak unto them. And it came to pass that he began to speak to his people from the tower; and they could not all hear his words beause of the greatness of the multitude; therefore he caused that the words which he spake should be written and sent forth among those that were not under the sound of his voice, that they might also receive his words." (Mosiah 2:7-8).

"Because I said unto you that I had spent my days in your service, I do not desire to boast, for I have only been in the service of God." (Mosiah 2:16).

"I, even I, whom ye call your king, am no better than ye yourselves are; for I am also of the dust. And ye behold that I am old, and am about to yield up this mortal frame to its mother earth." (Mosiah 2:26).

"Men drink damnation to their own souls except they humble themselves and become as little children, and believe that salvation was, and is, and is to come, in and through the atoning blood of Christ, the Lord Omnipotent. For the natural man is an enemy to God, and has been from the fall of Adam, and will be, forever and ever, unless he yields to the enticings of the Holy Spirit, and putteth off the natural man and becometh a saint through the atonement of Christ the Lord, and becometh as a child."
(Mosiah 3:18-19).

"I say unto you, if ye have come to a knowledge of the goodness of God, and his matchless power, and his wisdom, and his patience, and his long-suffering towards the children of men; and also, the atonement which has been prepared from the foundation of the world, that thereby salvation might come to him that should put his trust in the Lord, and should be diligent in keeping his commandments, and continue in the faith even unto the end of his life, I mean the life of the mortal body — I say, that this is the man who receiveth salvation, through the atonement which was prepared from the foundation of the world for all mankind, which ever were since the fall of Adam, or who are, or who ever shall be, even unto the end of the world." (Mosiah 4:6-7).

"If God, who has created you, on whom you are dependent for your lives and for all that ye have and are, doth grant unto you whatsoever ye ask that is right, in faith, believing that ye shall receive, O then, how ye ought to impart of the substance that ye have one to another."
(Mosiah 4:21).

"I give
not because
I have not, but if
I had, I would give."
(Mosiah 4:24).

"And see that all these things are done in wisdom and order; for it is not requisite that a man should run faster than he has strength. And again, it is expedient that he should be diligent, that thereby he might win the prize; therefore, all things must be done in order." (Mosiah 4:27).

"And now, because of the covenant which ye have made, ye shall be called the children of Christ, his sons, and his daughters; for behold, this day he hath spiritually begotten you; for ye say that your hearts are changed through faith on his name; therefore, ye are born of him and have become his sons and his daughters." (Mosiah 5:7).

"Whosoever shall not take upon him the name of Christ must be called by some other name; therefore, he findeth himself on the left hand of God. And I would that ye should remember also, that this is the name that I said I should give unto you that never should be blotted out of your hearts. I say unto you, I would that ye should remember to retain the name written always in your hearts, that ye are not found on the left hand of God, but that ye hear and know the voice by which ye shall be called, and also the name by which he shall call you."
(Mosiah 5:10-12).

"I will visit them in my anger. Yea, in my fierce anger will I visit them." (Mosiah 12:1).

"It is not expedient that we should have a king; for thus saith the Lord: Ye shall not esteem one flesh above another, or one man shall not think himself above another; therefore, I say unto you it is not expedient that ye should have a king." (Mosiah 23:7).

"Four of them were the sons of Mosiah; and their names were Ammon, and Aaron, and Omner, and Himni; these were the names of the sons of Mosiah." (Mosiah 27:34).

"He did deliver them because they did humble themselves before him; and because they cried mightily unto him he did deliver them out of bondage." (Mosiah 29:20).

"Did not my father Alma believe in the words which were delivered by the mouth of Abinadi? And was he not a holy prophet? Did he not speak the words of God, and my father Alma believe them?" (Alma 5:11).

"They are made known unto me by the Holy Spirit of God. Behold, I have fasted and prayed many days that I might know these things of myself. And now I do know of myself that they are true; for the Lord God hath made them manifest unto me by his Holy Spirit." (Alma 5:46).

"The angel said unto me he is a holy man; wherefore I know he is a holy man because it was said by an angel of God." (Alma 10:9).

"Zeezrom lay sick at Sidom, with a burning fever, which was caused by the great tribulations of his mind on account of his wickedness, for he supposed that Alma and Amulek were no more; and he supposed that they had been slain because of his iniquity. And this great sin, and his many other sins, did harrow up his mind until it did become exceedingly sore, having no deliverance; therefore, he began to be scorched with a burning heat." (Alma 15:3).

"He had slain many of them, because their brethren had scattered their flocks at the place of water; and thus, because they had had their flocks scattered, they were slain."
(Alma 18:6).

"Now when Alma had said these words, Korihor was struck dumb, that he could not have utterance, according to the words of Alma." (Alma 30:50).

"For it is expedient that an atonement should be made; for according to the great plan of the Eternal God there must be an atonement made, or else all mankind must unavoidably perish; yea, all are hardened; yea, all are fallen and are lost, and must perish except it be through the atonement which it is expedient should be made."
(Alma 34:9).

"For it is expedient that there should be a great and last sacrifice; yea, not a sacrifice of man, neither of beast, neither of any manner of fowl; for it shall not be a human sacrifice; but it must be an infinite and eternal sacrifice." (Alma 34:10).

"Now Alma, being grieved
for the iniquity of his people, yea
for the wars, and the bloodsheds, and
the contentions which were among them;
and having been to declare the word, or sent
to declare the word, among all the people in
every city; and seeing that the hearts of the
people began to wax hard, and that they
began to be offended because of the
strictness of the word, his heart
was exceedingly sorrowful."
(Alma 35:15)

"For they were in bondage, and none could deliver them except it was the God of Abraham, and the God of Isaac, and the God of Jacob; and he surely did deliver them in their afflictions." (Alma 36:2).

"The meaning of the word restoration is to bring back again ... good for that which is good; righteous for that which is righteous; just for that which is just; merciful for that which is merciful ... ye shall have mercy restored unto you again; ye shall have justice restored unto you again; ye shall have a righteous judgment restored unto you again; and ye shall have good rewarded unto you again."
(Alma 41:13-14).

"And he hath power given unto him from the Father to redeem them from their sins because of repentance; therefore he hath sent his angels to declare the tidings of the conditions of repentance, which bringeth unto the power of the Redeemer, unto the salvation of their souls."
(Helaman 5:11).

"The Nephites ... had become hardened and impenitent and grossly wicked, insomuch that they did reject the word of God and all the preaching and prophesying which did come among them. Nevertheless, the people of the church did have great joy because of the conversion of the Lamanites, yea, because of the church of God, which had been established among them. And they did fellowship one with another, and did rejoice one with another, and did have great joy."
(Helaman 6:2-3).

"Now the land south was called Lehi, and the land north was called Mulek, which was after the son of Zedekiah; for the Lord did bring Mulek into the land north, and Lehi into the land south."
(Helaman 6:10).

"Behold, now we will know of a surety whether this man be a prophet and God hath commanded him to prophesy such marvelous things unto us. Behold, we do not believe that he hath; yea, we do not believe that he is a prophet; nevertheless, if this thing which he has said concerning the chief judge be true, that he be dead, then will we believe that the other words which he has spoken are true." (Helaman 9:2).

"Behold, I give unto you power, that whatsoever ye shall seal on earth shall be sealed in heaven; and whatsoever ye shall loose on earth shall be loosed in heaven; and thus shall ye have power among this people." (Helaman 10:7).

"If we should go up against them, the Lord would deliver us into their hands; therefore, we will prepare ourselves in the center of our lands, and we will gather all our armies together, and we will not go against them, but we will wait till they shall come against us; therefore, as the Lord liveth, if we do this he will deliver them into our hands."
(3 Nephi 3:21).

"Your burnt offerings shall be done away, for I will accept none of your sacrifices and your burnt offerings." (3 Nephi 9:19).

"And it was the more righteous part of the people who were saved, and it was they who received the prophets and stoned them not; and it was they who had not shed the blood of the saints, who were spared." (3 Nephi 10:12).

"He that hath the spirit of contention is not of me, but is of the devil, who is the father of contention, and he stirreth up the hearts of men to contend with anger, one with another." (3 Nephi 11:29).

"No man can serve two masters; for either he will hate the one and love the other, or else he will hold to the one and despise the other. Ye cannot serve God and Mammon." (3 Nephi 13:24).

"Other sheep I have which are not of this fold; them also I must bring, and they shall hear my voice; and there shall be one fold, and one shepherd." (3 Nephi 15:17).

"I would speak somewhat unto the remnant of this people who are spared, if it so be that God may give unto them my words, that they may know of the things of their fathers; yea, I speak unto you, ye remnant of the house of Israel; and these are the words which I speak." (Mormon 7:1).

"Are not the things that God hath wrought marvelous in our eyes? Yea, and who can comprehend the marvelous works of God?" (Mormon 9:16).

"It was by faith that the three disciples obtained a promise that they should not taste of death; and they obtained not the promise until after their faith." (Ether 12:17).

"The manner of their elders and priests administering the flesh and blood of Christ unto the church; and they administered it according to the commandments of Christ; wherefore we know the manner to be true; and the elder or priest did minister it." (Moroni 4:1).

"I, Mormon, speak unto you, my beloved brethren; and it is by the grace of God the Father, and our Lord Jesus Christ, and his holy will, because of the gift of his calling unto me, that I am permitted to speak unto you at this time."
(Moroni 7:2).

Appendix One

Parallel poetry
in The Book of Mormon

Scriptures by Category

Antithetical Parallelism

1 Nephi 2:20-21	2 Nephi 9:23-24	Alma 22:6
1 Nephi 6:5	2 Nephi 9:39	Alma 33:21
1 Nephi 13:18	2 Nephi 12:5	Alma 36:20
1 Nephi 14:7	2 Nephi 12:7	Alma 36:21
1 Nephi 14:25	2 Nephi 13:24	Helaman 7:29
1 Nephi 15:3	2 Nephi 15:12	3 Nephi 13:34
1 Nephi 15:8-9	2 Nephi 15:15-16	3 Nephi 14:13
1 Nephi 16:3	2 Nephi 16:9	3 Nephi 20:42
1 Nephi 16:29	2 Nephi 16:10	3 Nephi 27:33
1 Nephi 17:6	2 Nephi 18:10	Mormon 1:16
1 Nephi 17:37	2 Nephi 18:19	Mormon 2:13
1 Nephi 17:38	2 Nephi 19:2	Mormon 2:14
1 Nephi 17:45	2 Nephi 21:3-4	Mormon 2:26
1 Nephi 19:7	2 Nephi 25:20	Ether 4:18
1 Nephi 21:7	2 Nephi 33:8	Ether 12:12
2 Nephi 1:7	Jacob 1:14	Ether 12:25
2 Nephi 1:20	Jacob 6:3	Ether 12:26
2 Nephi 1:25	Omni 1:3	Moroni 7:11
2 Nephi 1:26	Omni 1:25	Moroni 7:16-17
2 Nephi 1:28-29	Mosiah 2:25	Moroni 7:42
2 Nephi 2:11	Mosiah 3:29	Moroni 8:8
2 Nephi 2:28-29	Mosiah 18:21	
2 Nephi 3:17	Mosiah 27:29	
2 Nephi 4:4	Alma 1:25	
2 Nephi 4:19	Alma 5:40	
2 Nephi 4:33	Alma 9:13	
2 Nephi 9:16	Alma 9:28	

Synonymous Parallelism

1 Nephi 1:6-7	2 Nephi 7:3	Helaman 12:6
1 Nephi 2:3	2 Nephi 8:3	Helaman 13:11
1 Nephi 2:11	2 Nephi 9:52	Helaman 14:25
1 Nephi 5:19	2 Nephi 15:20	3 Nephi 2:1
1 Nephi 8:2	2 Nephi 22:4	3 Nephi 5:21
1 Nephi 9:4	2 Nephi 25:15	3 Nephi 6:18
1 Nephi 11:11	2 Nephi 28:3	3 Nephi 12:19
1 Nephi 11:21	2 Nephi 30:16	3 Nephi 16:20
1 Nephi 11:32	Jacob 1:6	3 Nephi 20:39
1 Nephi 12:2	Omni 1:12-13	Mormon 1:1
1 Nephi 12:4	Words of	Mormon 1:2
1 Nephi 17:36	Mormon 1:7	Mormon 3:15
1 Nephi 17:39	Mosiah 2:2	Mormon 3:16
1 Nephi 17:47	Mosiah 16:10	Mormon 4:5
1 Nephi 17:50	Mosiah 21:26	Mormon 9:9
1 Nephi 17:53-54	Mosiah 23:5	Mormon 9:10
1 Nephi 18:17-18	Mosiah 23:21	Ether 12:31
1 Nephi 18:34	Mosiah 24:23	Ether 14:2
1 Nephi 20:10	Alma 2:22	Moroni 2:7
1 Nephi 21:2	Alma 5:45	Moroni 7:13
1 Nephi 21:9	Alma 8:4	Moroni 8:17
1 Nephi 21:11	Alma 11:20	Moroni 10:6
1 Nephi 21:14	Alma 25:12	
1 Nephi 21:24	Alma 27:22	
2 Nephi 1:13	Alma 34:32	
2 Nephi 4:11	Alma 37:5	
2 Nephi 4:35	Alma 40:23	

Synthetic Parallelism

1 Nephi 1:1-2	2 Nephi 9:52	Alma 22:15
1 Nephi 1:15	2 Nephi 10:2	Alma 42:13
1 Nephi 3:3	2 Nephi 10:6	Alma 49:18
1 Nephi 9:2	2 Nephi 10:9	Alma 53:1
1 Nephi 11:2-5	2 Nephi 10:16	Helaman 6:17
1 Nephi 15:10	2 Nephi 10:19	3 Nephi 13:22
1 Nephi 15:15	2 Nephi 10:20	3 Nephi 14:6
1 Nephi 16:2	2 Nephi 10:22	3 Nephi 15:21
1 Nephi 17:11	2 Nephi 10:25	3 Nephi 16:3
1 Nephi 17:35	2 Nephi 11:3	3 Nephi 19:6
1 Nephi 19:23	2 Nephi 11:5	3 Nephi 23:3
1 Nephi 20:13	2 Nephi 11:7	3 Nephi 27:13
1 Nephi 21:25	2 Nephi 25:2	3 Nephi 30:2
2 Nephi 2:12	2 Nephi 25:4	4 Nephi 1:5
2 Nephi 2:25	2 Nephi 26:25	Mormon 1:18-19
2 Nephi 4:15-16	2 Nephi 29:7	Mormon 2:39
2 Nephi 4:17	Jacob 1:1	Mormon 8:25-26
2 Nephi 4:18	Enos 1:1	Mormon 9:11
2 Nephi 4:21	Omni 1:26	Ether 6:10
2 Nephi 4:23	Mosiah 2:9	Ether 12:26
2 Nephi 4:26	Mosiah 12:1	Moroni 7:12
2 Nephi 4:28	Mosiah 14:5	
2 Nephi 4:31-32	Mosiah 16:10	
2 Nephi 9:9	Alma 5:61	
2 Nephi 9:13	Alma 6:5	
2 Nephi 9:18	Alma 9:8	
2 Nephi 9:25-26	Alma 11:4	

Climactic Parallelism

1 Nephi 2:5	2 Nephi 9:6-7	Alma 32:14
1 Nephi 3:7	2 Nephi 9:12	Alma 36:4
1 Nephi 7:10-12	2 Nephi 9:25	Alma 42:14
1 Nephi 9:6	2 Nephi 9:26	Helaman 10:6
1 Nephi 10:2-3	2 Nephi 10:3	3 Nephi 6:13
1 Nephi 10:19	2 Nephi 20:17	3 Nephi 8:16
1 Nephi 15:33	2 Nephi 21:12	3 Nephi 10:15
1 Nephi 16:20	2 Nephi 23:10	Mormon 3:9-10
1 Nephi 17:19	2 Nephi 25:24-27	Mormon 3:12
1 Nephi 17:31	2 Nephi 25:29	Mormon 8:14
1 Nephi 18:2	2 Nephi 30:11	Ether 2:17
1 Nephi 18:22	2 Nephi 33:6	Ether 4:12
1 Nephi 19:15-17	Jacob 4:10	Ether 12:27
1 Nephi 19:24	Enos 1:4-5	Ether 12:32
1 Nephi 20:18	Mosiah 2:17	Ether 13:17
1 Nephi 20:21	Mosiah 10:17	Ether 14:1
2 Nephi 1:5	Mosiah 11:28	Moroni 7:8
2 Nephi 1:13-14	Mosiah 16:12	Moroni 7:35
2 Nephi 2:5-6	Mosiah 22:4	Moroni 7:44 & 46
2 Nephi 2:6-9	Mosiah 27:14	Moroni 10:32
2 Nephi 2:13	Mosiah 29:40	Moroni 10:33
2 Nephi 2:18	Alma 5:37	
2 Nephi 2:27	Alma 7:12	
2 Nephi 4:15-16	Alma 16:1	
2 Nephi 4:30	Alma 31:5	
2 Nephi 5:7	Alma 32:12	
2 Nephi 5:25	Alma 32:13	

Chiasmus

1 Nephi 1:16	2 Nephi 28:21	Alma 34:9
1 Nephi 1:17	2 Nephi 29:13	Alma 34:10
1 Nephi 2:4	Jacob 4:9	Alma 35:15
1 Nephi 3:5-6	Enos 1:8-9 & 11-12	Alma 36:2
1 Nephi 3:16	Enos 1:27	Alma 41:13-14
1 Nephi 6:1	Jarom 1:4	Helaman 5:11
1 Nephi 10:19	Omni 1:14	Helaman 6:2-3
1 Nephi 11:32	Mosiah 2:7-8	Helaman 6:10
1 Nephi 12:19	Mosiah 2:16	Helaman 9:2
1 Nephi 13:42	Mosiah 2:26	Helaman 10:7
1 Nephi 15:25	Mosiah 3:18-19	3 Nephi 3:21
1 Nephi 16:18	Mosiah 4:6-7	3 Nephi 9:19
1 Nephi 17:13	Mosiah 4:21	3 Nephi 10:12
1 Nephi 17:52	Mosiah 4:24	3 Nephi 11:29
1 Nephi 21:1	Mosiah 4:27	3 Nephi 13:24
1 Nephi 22:26	Mosiah 5:7	3 Nephi 15:17
2 Nephi 4:28-30	Mosiah 5:10-12	Mormon 7:1
2 Nephi 4:34	Mosiah 12:1	Mormon 9:16
2 Nephi 5:19	Mosiah 23:7	Ether 12:27
2 Nephi 6:16-17	Mosiah 27:34	Moroni 4:1
2 Nephi 9:20	Mosiah 29:20	Moroni 7:2
2 Nephi 9:28-29	Alma 5:11	
2 Nephi 15:25	Alma 5:46	
2 Nephi 16:10	Alma 10:9	
2 Nephi 22:2	Alma 15:3	
2 Nephi 24:12-15	Alma 18:6	
2 Nephi 24:29-31	Alma 30:50	

Appendix Two

Resources

"Poetic Parallelisms in The Book of Mormon: The Complete Text Reformatted" Donald W. Parry, Author. BYU Neal A. Maxwell Institute for Religious Scholarship. Maxwell Institute Publications. Available at: Scholarsarchive.byu.edu/mi/61/

See:
ChiasmusResources.org

chiasmusresources.org/index-chiasm-book-mormon#1 for a comprehensive list of chiasms in The Book of Mormon, that have been proposed by a number of Latter-day Saint scholars.

About The Author

Phil Hudson and his wife Jan have 7 children and over 25 grandchildren. They enjoy spending time with their family at their cabin nestled in the Selkirk Mountains, on the shore of Priest Lake, the crown jewel of North Idaho. Phil had a successful dental practice in Spokane, Washington for 43 years, before retiring in 2015. He has an eclectic mix of hobbies, and enjoys the out of doors. He always finds time, however, to record his thoughts on his laptop, and understands Isaac Asimov's response when he was asked: If you knew that you had only 10 minutes left to live, what would you do?" He answered: "I'd type faster."

Phil received the inspiration to write this book while he and Jan were serving as missionaries for The Church of Jesus Christ of Latter-day Saints, in the Kingdom of Tonga. While there, they celebrated their 50th wedding anniversary.

By The Author

Essays

    Volume One: Spray From The Ocean Of Thought
    Volume Two: Ripples On A Pond
    Volume Three: Serendipitous Meanderings
    Volume Four: Presents Of Mind
    Volume Five: Mental Floss
    Volume Six: Fitness Training For The Mind And Spirit

First Principles and Ordinances Series

    Faith - Our Hearts Are Changed
    Repentance - A Broken Heart and a Contrite Spirit
    Baptism - One Hundred And One Reasons Why We Are Baptized
    The Holy Ghost - That We Might Have His Spirit To Be With Us
    The Sacrament - This Do In Remembrance Of Me

Book of Mormon Commentary

    Volume One: Born In The Wilderness
    Volume Two: Voices From The Dust
    Volume Three: Journey To Cumorah

Doctrine & Covenants Commentary

    Volume One - Sections 1 - 34
    Volume Two - Sections 35 - 57

Minute Musings: Spontaneous Combustions of Thought

    Volume One
    Volume Two
    Volume Three

Calendars:

    In His Own Words: Discovering William Tyndale
    As I Think About The Savior
    Scriptural Symbols

Children's Books

    The Hiawatha Trail: An Allegory
    Book of Mormon Hiking Song
    Happy Birthday
    Muddy, Muddy
    The Parable of The Pencil
    The Little Princess
    The Thirteen Articles of Faith

Doctrinal Themes

- Are Christians Mormon?
- Christmas is The Season When…
- Dentistry in The Scriptures
- Gratitude
- Hebrew Poetry
- Hiding in Plain Sight
- Ninety Nine Questions Answered by The Book of Mormon……
- The House of The Lord
- Without The Book of Mormon
- Writing on Metal Plates

A Thought For Each Day of the Year

- Faith
- Repentance
- Baptism
- The Holy Ghost
- The Sacrament
- The House of the Lord
- The Plan of Salvation
- The Atonement
- Revelation
- The Sabbath
- Life's Greatest Questions

Professional Publications

- Diode Laser Soft Tissue Surgery Volume One
- Diode Laser Soft Tissue Surgery Volume Two
- Diode Laser Soft Tissue Surgery Volume Three

These, and other titles, are available from online retailers.

Quid magis possum dicere?